Off Track

Or How I Dropped Out of College and Came to be a Horse Trainer in the 70s While All My Friends were Still Doing Drugs

Jim McGarrah

Blue Heron Book Works

Cover design by Angie Zambrano

Blue Heron Book Works, LLC
Allentown, Pennsylvania
www.blueheronbookworks.com

This book is a work of nonfiction in that it is a personal recollection of events I have been intimately associated with during a particular era of my life. It is neither journalism, nor a history textbook. Some names have been changed to protect the innocent. More names have been changed to protect the not so innocent.

This book is dedicated to John Bill

(1921-1998)

"There is finally the pride of thinking oneself without teachers.
The teachers are everywhere. What is wanted is a learner.
In ignorance is hope.
Rely on ignorance. It is ignorance the teachers will come to.
They are waiting, as they always have, beyond the edge of the light."

-Wendell Berry

Table of Contents

Thanks to these magazines and presses for publishing portions of this book:

Amarillo Bay Review

Bayou Magazine

The Bitter Southerner

Breakwater

Chamber Four Magazine

Elixir

Hamilton Stone Review

Home Again: Essays and Memoirs from Indiana

Ink Brush Press

North American Review

Open 24 Hours

Southern Indiana Review

Traces Magazine

Under the Sun

Introduction

The Only Kentucky Race Track in Indiana

My father's thick hand holds a shiny quarter just out of reach. He laughs, flicking it in the air with his thumb and forefinger. The silver shimmers in the blue sky. I wait for the sun to spit it back at me.

"Take that money and buy us a racing program. I'm going to get a ticket on the daily double. I'm going to buy you one too."

"I haven't picked any horses, dad."

"That's alright. We'll get a four and an eight. You were born ten years ago in '48."

Whenever I drive by Ellis Park Race Track, I remember that scene. Those two horses lost their respective races, of course. Over a forty-year span, from that dog day afternoon in 1958 to the present, so have many others, saddled with my father's pari-mutuel tickets. He was a great handicapper but, a terrible gambler. Dad read the statistics in *The Racing Form* better than any horseman I ever knew. Not only that, we could watch the thoroughbreds prance through the paddock before each race and I believe, to this very day, he understood their thoughts.

"See the white foam around the saddle girth on that number 4 horse?"

"Yeah. It looks like whipped cream."

"That's sweat. That horse is washing out. I remember him the last time he ran. He wasn't nervous. There's something bothering him today."

"What. What's bothering him?"

"It doesn't matter. Something, anything. He just won't run good. But, look at the muscle tone on the number three horse. See how he's trying to push his groom around. See how he's up on the bit. He looks good in *The Racing Form* too. That horse'll run big."

More often than not, my father's analytical skills and observations proved true. Many of those horses did run very well, but not with his money on them. He only bet to win, never place, never show. The idea that the best horse might encounter uncontrollable circumstances and not win was a foreign one. Dad held the same view for horseracing, for baseball, and for life.

"Place bets are for sissies. If the horse's good enough to run second, he's good enough to win," he always said, as it broke bad, ran up behind a wall of other horses, or got pulled by the jockey. Then, without questioning the weakness of his logic, he would rip the useless ticket in half and begin the ritual anew, buying a win ticket on another horse in the next race. One day in the late 1970's, when I was grown and operating a successful racing stable of my own, my father sat on a park bench at Ellis and picked eight horses in eight races that ran second. It was a remarkable feat; yet, he never cashed a single ticket.

These memories flood my mind forty years later. I'm walking through the cavernous old concrete grandstand toward the Racing Secretary's office. Even though the meet has been closed since August and my father died last month, I still taste homemade relish on the polish sausages. I hear the crowd rise to its feet on the balcony above me, screaming for a one thousand pound animal to stick his nose in front of another at an invisible wire on a clay track. I feel the ground vibrate as forty hooves drum down the stretch. For an instant, the air seems electric, swirling and crackling, like a jockey's whip has just sliced through it. The smell of leather and sweat is everywhere.

Then there is silence and a brisk autumn breeze.

I left the racing game for good in 1982 when my second child was born. I like to tell myself that I'm a good person, that I left the grueling lifestyle to properly raise children. We all stroke our conscience occasionally. The real reason was much less altruistic. The thrill of horse racing kept me sane after I returned from Vietnam. I loved the game. I loved shipping from one bush league track to another, working like a gypsy seven days a week. I loved the cool mornings when dawn was a mist rising from the compost and the air reeked of Bigel oil and bad coffee. Most of all, I loved the adrenalin that accelerated my heart each time one of our stable's thoroughbreds turned for home with his neck in front of the field.

When the things I loved began to fade, overwhelmed by a concern for tax laws, a search for corporate sponsors, a desire for gimmick bets, and a need for the attitude of a carnival shill, I wanted a way out. Familial responsibility provided it. But, when you abandon something you enjoy, there is a tinge of regret that becomes a permanent part of who you are. An era ends in your mind long before your heart accepts its fate.

I'm feeling this regret in the pit of my stomach right now as I enter Bobby Jackson's new office. I've come here months after the summer meet has ended on a late autumn day at the beginning of the 21st century to discuss the current state of racing at this track and to write a magazine article about it. But my heart wants more than information. It wants vindication. I want him to tell me I was right, leaving the game when I did. His confirmation that Ellis Park, a racing facility that lasted more than sixty years as a family owned enterprise, has surrendered its county fair atmosphere and Hoosier farmland values to the slick corporate demeanor of its new buyer Churchill Downs, will go a long way in justifying the decision I made to leave behind something I loved.

Although this is my story, it is bigger than my story. I belonged to a more romantic time. I believed in the idea of horse racing as more than a business, more than a job. Almost religious in a way, racing was a calling to me, a way of life, and the people in my story lived and felt the same kinship with horses that I did. As our society in America began to emphasize money as the sole reason for "doing" anything, that concept naturally seeped into the horse business. The nobility, the art – my main interests – faded and the desire for profit surpassed the enjoyment of sport. The substance of my life became only form. Now, I would see for myself the external changes that correspond with my attitude. Now, I would have a tangible touchstone to compare with my memory.

Chapter One

The Tale of How Monk Johnson Found Redemption at Churchill Downs

Red Harvey had only one ear on his head. The other found its way into a trash bin behind the track kitchen at Churchill Downs, bitten off and spit out by Monk Johnson after a fifth ace appeared in Red's poker deck during a Monk Johnson losing streak. This all occurred at the spring race meet in 1972, the year Red Harvey got religion. During the attack, Monk heard Red scream, "Bless you, Brother Monk." Red had always believed that the devil was trying to suck his soul out through his right ear because of the ringing he often heard after a hard night of vodka drinking. It was a simple leap of faith for Red to assume that Monk might be making a gesture of salvation.

Part of the reason for Red's misunderstanding of Monk's intentions may have been the fact that Monk was in charge of the night security guard detail. He wore an orange vest over his uniform so drunk drivers could avoid him while he prowled the barn area in his golf cart looking for drunk drivers. The vest gave off a glow in the headlights that surrounded Monk with a corona, much like the one that surrounded the picture of Jesus that Monk kept taped to the dash of his cart. In fact, Monk was aware of this phenomenon and did all he could to encourage it. The air of divinity it created seemed helpful in reminding everyone of his importance.

Convinced that his left ear was the sacrifice that saved his soul, Red strutted through the barn area for weeks after the fight in a turban of white gauze, casting out demons and blessing crippled horses. Some of the jockeys called him "Swami Red" and bowed gracefully when he passed. But whenever Red stopped to thank Monk for taking the ear and blessing him with salvation, Monk just spit and growled, "You're gonna pay for what you done to me."

It seems that when the paramedic brought him to the emergency room, the docs found out Red's eardrum was busted and he couldn't hear a thing on that left side. Monk had popped him upside the head real good with a cafeteria tray before deciding to have the ear for a snack. The docs were worried about who was going to pay the medical bills for all the work they were doing on Red's head and they called The Horsemen's Benevolent and Protective Society. The Society agreed to foot the bill, but wanted a detailed description of the incident for their records. Evidently, Red could be eloquent when called upon. He described Monk's charitable action so well that, when called in to give his side of the story, all Monk could do was agree with the account, except the part about him being Jesus, of course. He would never want to appear as crazy as old Red Harvey. The members of the Horsemen's Society filed a formal complaint against Monk with his superiors. His wages were garnished every week to pay for Red's medical care. His official golf cart was taken away and he got demoted to walking the track between 10 p.m. and 6 a.m. It wasn't fair at all, considering that Red Harvey had been the cheater and had even given Monk a black eye before someone had opened the back door of the kitchen and tossed a pail of cold water on them both.

On the other hand, having his hearing halved invigorated Red's spiritual power in ways Monk could not fully comprehend. But, Monk knew from the first time he'd been laid at the age of twelve that a person didn't have to understand how something worked to use it. Scriptures that Monk hadn't heard since childhood in church spewed constantly from Red Harvey's mouth. Monk would often hear Red preaching in the track kitchen when he took his early morning coffee break. Eventually, Monk stopped coming to the track kitchen because he felt embarrassed when Red would wail upon seeing him, "Praise God for Monk Johnson. The man who brought me salvation."

As Monk withered with rage, Red blossomed. A clarity of purpose formed. He quit drinking so much vodka. Once, when he poured cinnamon on his oatmeal, it was rumored the brown specs outlined the face of Jesus. The old mutts that hung around the barns looking for scraps began to follow him. Children begged to touch his bandaged head. Monk swore revenge. To him, Red Harvey became the focal point of every misfortune that followed their fight. When his hemorrhoids flared, when he lost his paycheck on a sure winner, and when a wisdom tooth impacted, Monk linked each event to Red's spiritual ascendance.

Three weeks to the day after the ear had been chewed off, Monk stopped by the Horseman's Bar to buy a trifecta ticket on the third race. He had a good tip from one of the trainers and was sure he was about to become a rich man. The Horseman's Bar wasn't really the name of the place. It didn't have a name. Monk just called it that because it made him feel more important. When his family asked him where he was off to, he always said the Horsemen's Bar as if he were more than a security guard who worked at the pleasure of real horse people.

The bar stretched along the back wall beneath the grandstand seats at the end of the long tunnel into the paddock where the horses were saddled before each race. It derived its nickname from being the closest place for a horse trainer to buy a drink after sending his thoroughbred onto the track. The area came complete with a mirror, flashing neon beer signs, shelves of various bourbons, scotches, vodkas, and gins and a black-tied bartender. The crowd seemed almost like an evangelical congregation. There was constant inquiring after the health and welfare of various members. The Daily Racing Form was read and discussed like scripture in a Sunday school class. Everyone kept his or her nose in everyone else's business, and when the horses rounded the quarter pole and headed for the wire, whooping, hollering and other strange noises, like talking in tongues, echoed off the cavernous concrete walls.

Monk's three horses finished up the track. As he ripped his ticket to shreds and started to leave, old Red came running away from the cashier's window and into the bar with a handful of hundred dollar bills. He carried his head tilted to the left side as if protecting the blank space where his ear used to be from the wind rushing by and he leaned forward when he ran, like his upper torso was falling and his legs struggled to get underneath it and catch it.

"What I won. What I won," he said. "I just won six thousand dollars on the trifecta. Set'em up barkeep. Cold Duck for all my friends."

"Red, you know we don't keep fancy wine here," said the bartender, handing Red a double shot of vodka. Red laid a hundred dollar bill on the bar.

"Tell me when this runs out. I got more, my man, a lot more. The Lord works in mysterious ways his wonders to perform. Praise God." Red looked at Monk. Monk shuddered and quietly cursed.

"Are you a preacher?" A soft voice curled around the back of Red's head entwined with the pale blue cigar smoke. He turned toward the sound. A frail woman who looked to be in her mid-thirties, but was probably much younger, smiled directly into his eyes. Her eyelids were heavy and her mouth slightly uneven. She had teased a full head of reddish-brown hair into an imitation Afro and with her red mini-skirt and white halter-top wasn't half bad looking in a used sort of way. Most of the horsemen knew her as the pro named Jane who had given Freddie Merchant, one of the starting gate workers, a dose of clap two weeks before. Monk should have run her out the back gate, but he decided to let nature take its course. There was always the possibility Red Harvey could end up with the clap.

"Why little lady, I am a Christian, and every Christian who's a real one is a preacher," said Red. "The Lord don't let sinners win the trifecta."

She slid past the bartender and snuggled next to Red with an animal grace, both vulnerable and dangerous like a wounded bird of prey, and placed her hand over Red's missing ear. "They say you can save people from themselves, even if they're really bad people."

"I can, little lady, I can."

Red drank another shot of vodka and slammed the glass upside down on the bar. He whirled around three hundred and sixty degrees, spit between his palms, and rubbed his hands together furiously. Everyone gathered in a tight circle so quiet you could hear a pari-mutuel ticket hit the floor. Red Harvey separated his hands above his head and brought them down on Jane's shoulders. Gripping her firmly, he shook her back and forth, chanting with his eyes closed, "Eli Eli La' Ma, Sa Bach Tha' ni." Then, he stepped back and clapped. "Begone from this angel, all you demons and creatures of Satan."

The bartender had refilled Red's glass. Trembling, Red reached for it and poured it down. He gave Jane a hundred dollar bill. "Let he among you who is without sin cast the first stone."

No one threw anything, not even Monk, although his face flushed as he thought of how he might get away with it. They all turned back to the bar and ordered another round of drinks just as the starter's bell clanged and the next race began.

***

Red and Jane were married the following week. She vowed to Red that she had seen the light right in front of Monk Johnson at the track kitchen. Monk felt overjoyed. Having been married twice before himself, he knew the agony awaiting Red Harvey. There was a huge ceremony on the backside of the racetrack in a little park by the tack shop. Someone brought two kegs of beer over in the back of his pickup truck and a couple of horse trainers roasted a whole hog on a spit. It was a hell of a party. The track chaplain who married them got drunk and puked in the front seat of his own Cadillac. Fred Merchant told everyone that Jane was a great gal and that he really caught the clap from a dirty toilet seat in Detroit. Monk came to the wedding for the free beer. Red had asked him to be the best man, but Monk refused. Red paid him back all the money he had won in the crooked poker game.

As a matter of fact, Red paid for the whole party and, when he began handing over his money to various people, Monk took Jane aside. "You know, you won't never see a penny unless you get Red real drunk and take it. Remember it's as much yours as his now, by law."

Jane smiled, placed her hand on Monk's crotch and gave him a friendly squeeze. "Thanks for the tip," she said.

A horse has to cool down immediately following physical exertion by walking and taking periodic sips of water. It doesn't take a rocket scientist to handle a leather lead shank and walk in a circle, and this was Red's job. He did it well. But his work started at the same time Monk's guard shift ended. Two days after the wedding, Monk watched Red leave his dormitory room and walk past the clocker's tower to Winston Jenkins' barn where he walked hot horses. Monk let himself in the room and woke Jane. He waved a twenty-dollar bill under her nose.

"You didn't close up the shop just because you got married, did you?" Jane drew the covers back and patted the empty spot on the cot, still warm from Red's body.

"It didn't get sewed up when I took them vows," she said.

After they finished, Monk helped her search the room for Red's money. It wasn't difficult to find. Monk figured that since Red believed his trifecta win was a gift from God, he would also believe that God protected it. When they found an old Bible in the footlocker, Monk held it upside down and shook. Hundred dollar bills rained from the gospels. He helped himself to a couple as a finder's fee and then placed the rest in Jane's purse. "I'm going to take you to the back gate and put you on the metro bus out to Standiford Field. I want you to catch a plane to Chicago and work the Arlington meet. Don't come back here, ever, or I'll have you busted."

"Why would I?"

Jane's leaving crushed poor old Red as surely as if a thousand pound stud horse had flipped over backward and landed on him, just like Monk hoped it would. He didn't seem to care that he was flat broke. The problem was that he still loved her. Monk knew that, but Red's suffering seemed justified, considering the misery he'd brought on Monk, although, it didn't bring the security guard the satisfaction he'd hoped for. Red's long face and constantly damp eyes made Monk feel guilty, so he bought a bottle of vodka for Red to sleep with as a gesture of goodwill. Red had no idea of Monk's complicity in Jane's treachery and thanked him for his kindness.

When the first bottle was gone, Red quit preaching and started wearing a stocking cap pulled low to cover the space where his ear had been. He drank the Dark Eyes vodka like water from the time he got up until the time he passed out at night. Sometimes, he didn't even get out of bed to piss. This binge might seem like no big deal because a lot of people on the racetrack drank too much vodka in those days.

However, Red's return to hard drinking soon became a big deal. The backside barn area was full of misfits, runaways, and people who simply had nowhere else to go. They formed a community of their own, and it was a pretty close-knit one, even though they traveled across the country from race meet to race meet. Like migratory birds of a feather, they flocked together, you might say. Through his evangelical message of faith, Red Harvey had been the hub, the center of this community. The preaching he had done every Sunday morning when he got off work made him magical. The hot walkers and the grooms, hungover, hungry, and in need of any message that might give them enough hope to get up for work on Monday, would congregate in the corner of the track kitchen and listen.

Like many people raised around fundamental Christians, Red Harvey could recite verse after verse from the Bible. He'd learned the scriptures at a Pentecostal orphanage where he'd spent his childhood. Also like many fundamental Christians, Red had no idea what the words meant. The sound the language made when it was chanted brought the spirit from somewhere in Heaven and gave the chanter religion. Consequently, his sermons often contained very little actual wisdom, but the rhythm seemed to animate the souls of the disconnected ones who listened. Monk began to realize that his revenge might be affecting more than one person. It was a result he hadn't planned on.

Red would shout, "Either make the tree good and its fruit good; or make the tree bad and its fruit bad; for the tree is known by its fruit. And we will cast all the fruits into the furnace of fire; there shall be weeping and gnashing of teeth, for verily I say unto ye, man shall not lie with man and spread his seed to the fruits. Behold, the Lord is riding on a swift cloud and the idols of Egypt will tremble at his presence when He comes into Jerusalem on his ass. Moreover, the manufacturers of linen made from combed flax and the weavers of white cloth will be utterly dejected." There would be a nodding of heads and a gentle collective sway in the congregation. Some of the married folk brought their babies up after the impromptu services to touch the scar tissue on the side of Red's head. It was said by many that the power emitted from the absence of the ear would cure everything from tonsillitis to genital warts.

This hopefulness had dissipated with Red's self-control. When the hooker left him, she took his will, and Monk watched Red take vodka to fill the empty spot till the vodka took him. He fell out of favor with his boss after he came in drunk to water the horses off and left the webbing unfastened one night on the stall door of a prize filly. The filly trotted out of the barn, got spooked by a manure truck backfiring, and took off at a dead run out of the back gate at Churchill Downs. Dodging the traffic on Fourth Street, the filly managed to skid on the gravel in the parking lot of Doc Harthill's vet clinic and crash into the plate glass window. She was cut up bad enough that her racing career ended right there before she'd ever earned enough money to pay her training bill.

Red was fired for his carelessness, he drank more Dark Eyes and quit showing up for Sunday morning service at the track kitchen. He quit showing up at the track kitchen at all. Some of the most faithful tried stopping him in the barn area and asking for spiritual advice. Red would scream at them, "Go fug youslef. I ain't nobody's prichur," and wobble away till they quit coming around.

Red Harvey was in the process of being ruled off the track for vagrancy when an old hard boot trainer named Winston Hughes hired him at the back gate. Monk even put in a good word for Red. Winston's only stable help was a kid who had let himself get bitten by a cheap stud on the way to the paddock for a 5,000 dollar claiming race. Winston had to have someone hold the horse while it got saddled, and Red was the only hand around.

Monk took Winston aside. "All this stuff happening to Red ain't his fault," he said to Winston. "Just give him a chance and he'll do right by you."

The horse won that race by four lengths. Red claimed it was because the stud liked little ginger drunks with only one ear, but Winston thought it was something that went deeper than that. Red could whisper in any horse's ear, stroke its neck, and get more out of the animal than it had to give. It was a mystery and hard boots have always been superstitious.

The honeymoon, so to speak, between Red and Winston lasted only three weeks, and then bales of hay started giving birth to empty Dark Eyes bottles. The tack room where Red slept at the end of the barn began giving off an odor of urine and vomit mixed with rolled oats, leather, and the black strap molasses Winston kept to spoon feed iron deficient horses. The stink made the other grooms and hot walkers reluctant to enter the shared room to retrieve equipment. Twice, Winston called Monk and two other guards into his barn because he couldn't wake Red and thought he was dead.

Red's work was passable, even admirable sometimes. Even when he was drunk, he would sit outside the barn on cool mornings while dawn was nothing more than a gray mist rising from the compost piles, the air filled with the reek of Bigel oil and bad coffee. When one of the horses came back from the track, lathered white and snorting from a sharp gallop, Red would jump up and hook the lead chain through the horse's halter and begin the walk. Of course, everyone did that. It was the *way* he did it that let you know he viewed hot walking as an art form rather than a job. He always rubbed the horse's nose and whispered things into its ear. His touch and his soft voice gave the animals the calm assurance that someone who really *cared* was caring for them. Even when he was drunk, which was pretty much all the time, Winston couldn't fault his work. It was his lifestyle that irritated everyone. One morning before everyone else came to work, Winston asked Monk to talk with Red.

"Red, you've got to clean yourself up." Monk said.

"Why?"

"You're stinking up the whole barn area. No one wants to go in there and no one wants to be around you. You stink, and besides, Johnny Wilson said you threw a bucket at him yesterday when he came in to get a bridle." Johnny Wilson was another hardboot that shared the barn with Winston.

"I was sleepin', and the little fucker tried to steal my bottle."

"Your bottle was under his bridle."

"A person's hands outta be specific when they reach for something."

"Well, here's the bottom line, Red. You need to quit drinking and take a shower on a regular basis or Winston's going to fire you. He don't want to, but he'll have to. Why don't you start reading the Bible again? Something in there might help you. You used to be well respected for your preaching, Red."

"I ain't touched the book since the woman left. Whatever magic was in the Bible, she took with her. All I got left with was the words. Man can't live by words alone. The spirit ain't in me no more, but I need to work. I'll do my best to leave off the booze."

***

Red had been showered, shaved, and on the wagon for three whole days when the delirium tremens hit him and Monk Johnson saved his life. It was a close night, one of those Kentucky summer nights that made you feel like you were walking near a volcano on the bottom of the ocean. The usual slight complaints rose from the blistered earth, crickets rubbed, fans hummed, truck tires crunched the gravel. Occasionally, a horse whinnied or a cat in heat squealed. It wasn't a vacuum, but the noise had divested itself of humanity, like a morgue. When Monk passed the clocking tower across from the six-furlong pole on the track during his nightly rounds, he stepped through the gap where horses entered the track during daylight training hours.

As he walked through the cupping sand surface on the main track, Monk began to sweat and wheeze. Above his labored breathing, a sound wound its way around his head. At first it was a dull hum like an electric transformer makes, but the closer he came to the nightlights in the grandstand, the more he could hear the one sound split into many and the intimate and individual sounds divide and fuse over and over until they became words. They cascaded down the empty bleachers and off the tin grandstand roof like raindrops, bouncing and marching down the track toward him. Finally, he saw the small, naked figure of Red Harvey standing in the circle beam produced by the large flashlight in Monk's hand. His clothes lay in a dirty heap on the ground behind him. The brightness seemed to blind Red, and he shielded his eyes with the palm of his right hand. He had picked the jockey scales at the finish line where the jockeys weighed in after every race to use as his stage.

"Mene Mene Tikel Parsin. I've been weighed on the scales and found deficient."

His body was covered with coarse red hair, even though he was almost completely bald, and his voice had a deep bass tremolo as he chanted a litany of scriptures that could only be connected somehow in his own mind. He did not see Monk.

"And as he journeyed, he came near Damascus, and suddenly there shined round about him a light from heaven, and he fell to the earth." Red Harvey dropped on all fours and touched his forehead to the metal scales. "And heard a voice say unto him, Saul, Saul why persecutest thou me? And he said, Who art thou, Lord? And the Lord said, I am Jesus whom thou persecutest: it is hard for thee to kick against the pricks. And he, trembling and astonished, said, what wilt thou have me to do?"

At this point, Red stood up and opened his arms as if to embrace the flashlight beam. In the pre-dawn hours of summer, it was uncommon for Churchill Downs to experience gusts of wind that kicked up the fine sand on the top layer of the racetrack. Oh, Monk had seen it happen frequently during the fall meeting in November, but summer breezes in Louisville, Kentucky were slight at best. Nevertheless, as Red opened his arms wide, the wind howled through the empty grandstand and over the track swirling sand and litter and uncashed pari-mutuel tickets together into tiny tornadoes. When Red raised his voice above the din and into the eerie gray light of coming morning, even Monk got a little frightened.

"And I looked and, behold a great cloud, and a fire infolding itself, and out of the midst of the flame there came the likeness of four living creatures and every one had four faces. Wheels rolled within wheels and my bones burned and a seven-headed beast rose up from the sea. It had ten horns and was ridden by a harlot, and Babylon the Great was her name until she got eaten by dogs with the swift taste for a Jezebel." Red fell to his knees weeping. "The pale horse rides. My God, my God, why hast Thou forsaken me. Jesus wept. I don't know the man. And, the cock crowed thrice."

Sadness overwhelmed Monk. A warm force in the morning wind he couldn't explain caressed him. Red's words brought tears to his eyes, and he felt, maybe for the first time in his life, that he might be part of a bigger plan, a scheme outside his own mind. It wasn't a huge feeling, but large enough that he put his walkie-talkie to his lips to call for the track ambulance instead of reaching for his billy club.

When Monk depressed the talk button, static crackled in the air and mingled with the wind. Red grew confused, seeking the source of the sound. He dropped his hands, stared into the light and whimpered, "I hear you calling Lord."

Monk saw an opening and, like a good race rider, drove for it. "Walk toward me in the light and thou shall be clothed in the blanket of a horse and carried away in my chariot to a room of white angels where thou shall be cured," he announced in his deepest voice.

"I'm afraid, Lord."

"Do not fear those who care for you. Only fear my wrath if you disobey."

"The beasts are all around me, Lord."

"I shall extinguish the light, and when you see the light again, two angels disguised as men you know shall take you in their arms and comfort you. The beasts will be gone."

The ambulance was making its way around the outside rail of

the track. Monk shook his head and clicked the flashlight off for a few seconds, and then clicked it back on. This time he shined the beam at Red's feet and drew it slowly toward the coming ambulance. Red Harvey followed the light.

***

I loved that story every time Dan Wilson got drunk and told it, which was frequently in 1976, the year after I quit fighting with my father long enough to ask for help getting a job and went to work grooming thoroughbred race horses on the Midwest racing circuit, the year my mind began to come home from the war. As I think about it now I realize the story appealed to my need for belonging because it was a personal story, the kind you shared during intimate moments at family gatherings about a wayward uncle or misfit cousin, the kind of narrative passed down from generation to generation in tribal mythology. I had felt lost since my discharge from the Marine Corps in 1969 and the goal of passing initiation into another special brotherhood gave my life purpose.

Not only that, but I knew Monk and Red Harvey. Both men still worked at various tracks on the Midwest racing circuit and I ran into them in this small, isolated world continually. How much of the story was true? Well, that was a question that could have been asked about anything spoken and many things seen at any race track. Red Harvey did have a missing ear and an ex-wife. Monk and he were as close as brothers and got drunk every day together. Monk had spent time as a security guard, and Red had been to rehab several times. Most importantly, neither man ever contradicted Dan Wilson or any other teller of this tale on the track.

Beyond the bond created by the narration, I relished the story sharing because I liked to watch Monk Johnson's face. The man turned crimson at various points no matter how many times or where Dan retold the incident. I always tried to guess whether the embarrassment came from the disclosure of Monk's pettiness or his compassion. Either one could hurt the reputation of a hard boot. Monk himself never said one way or the other. The guy rarely spoke about the incident himself unless he was drinking whiskey instead of beer. He had quit working as a security guard the day after Red Harvey's disappearance in the ambulance and took a job as a stable hand with Winston Connor's outfit. Monk hadn't done very much for the last four years but drink beer all day and muck stalls or cool out hot thoroughbreds after exercise, almost the same existence chosen by Red Harvey. Some old timers argued that the ambulance Dan claimed Monk had called wasn't real. They believed God transported Red somehow to a safe place but left a piece of his tormented soul, along with the ear, to possess the man who had injured him, caused his wife to leave, and interrupted his prophetic revelations that fateful night.

I never bought the idea of supernatural interference. An ambulance was always available on the backside of every race track, too many fights, too many drunks, too many accidents. No track could have gotten liability insurance without one. As far as I know, Red never once explained to anyone where he had been taken, or by what. He would say only that the lord had redeemed him. But the fact that Red vanished for a while and the reality that no one seemed to know exactly where he went once the ambulance drove away created an air of magic that excited me. I believed that if some enchantment was left in life, some romance, then it might be possible to survive ugly memories and generate enough positive energy to get from one day to the next in search of possibilities.

That's what life had become since my return from Vietnam, a constant struggle between memory and possibility. I needed the possibility of living a structured life on the outside so I could hold the inside together. The race track brought me that structure. Even though I traveled like a carnie around the country and even though my economic future was in constant doubt, I had a family that passed no judgment, a home isolated from the chaos in the rest of society, and a chance for redemption that had eluded me. As a lot of Viet vets, I had come to feel like a villain for engaging in acts I thought would make me a hero.

But first I needed to fall in love and the nearest racetrack was closed for the winter.

Chapter 2

The Road to Angst

Headline – Mexico Is Warm in the Winter

You can see something in its infancy and it appears completely forgettable such as an orchid bulb or a block of marble owned by Michelangelo. Then, you return much later to find a rare red Phalaenopsis has flowered or David stands in a pile of marble shavings. The transformations seem instantaneous, miraculous even, and you're amazed at your own stupidity for not noticing these exquisite creations before.

That happened to me with Eva, who I remembered as a scrawny child, freckled and puppy-clumsy, the little sister of one of my best high school friends. It was cold outside in the Indiana wind. I was bored inside. The wine was cheap. The pot was full of stems. My father spent his every waking minute reminding me that I had no drive, no purpose, no reason for living, and my attitude was un-American. An honorably discharged United States Marine should fulfill certain responsibilities in society. He never specified what those were.

Hard drugs had hurt us all in one way or another and we had laid them aside by the middle of the 1970's. This failure of our parents' generation to understand our "baby-boomer" angst marked the tenor of the conversation as I sat around a kitchen table with three of my closest childhood friends in Princeton, Indiana. We were celebrating my twenty-seventh birthday with a bottle of Ripple wine and a couple of joints. A woman a few years younger than the rest of us, a few inches taller than me, and blessed with a smile intense enough to lighten a black hole in some distant galaxy entered the room.

"I wish I could go somewhere warm," she said.

Where once threads of dark hair twisted their way around a pole between her head and shoulders, the god of puberty had spun a silk shawl that curled along her delicate pearl-colored neck. The pogo sticks she walked on were now elegant and graceful legs and each step she took, a ballet. The freckles that covered her face once now decorated the bridge of her nose as if stardust. Every single, hackneyed and nauseating phrase I had ever read in a Rod McKuen poem or saw on a Hallmark card paraded its way through the Swiss cheese that made up my drunken brain. The drunken delusional romanticism that had plagued my life before was at it once again. At the time, though, I knew only one thing. The ugly duckling had become Leda the Swan, and suddenly I wanted to play Zeus.

This was the infirmity I brought home from war, the inability to distinguish specific emotions, in this case the difference between love and desire. Because I had denied their existence in order to survive Vietnam, my spectrum of moods had atrophied and now I struggled to feel anything no matter how vague. On the occasions that I did feel a warm twinge in the back of my mind, I was never sure if it could be called an emotion or simply a reaction to my intellect warning me that I should feel something, *anything*.

"You'd like to go somewhere warm? I can arrange that, if you don't mind riding in an old pickup truck with two burned-out hippies."

"Sounds like fun," Eva said.

***

Sleeping bags and back packs, tie-dyed tee shirts and golden earrings, smoked oysters and Sterling beer, a dog-eared copy of *Death in the Afternoon* and a Rand McNally Atlas, one ancient Ford pickup truck and one balding, pony-tailed, be-speckled Jew whose constant good humor and kindness kept us sane driving through Kansas – these were the items Eva and I brought from Indiana. By nightfall we were well into Kansas, heading west and south at seventy miles an hour. The battered old truck rattled and shook, the wheels shimmied, the tires thumped like hoof beats, but we kept moving forward as if Tom Joad's ghost pushed us from behind. The sun had simply spread out like a pat of butter and melted into the dry toast landscape. I saw the same flat nothingness in the indigo night that I had seen during the day. The only difference was darkness. Joey slept against the passenger side door, his pony-tail rubbing a slick spot on the glass. I drove and stayed awake by focusing on the night sounds led by his snoring and the occasional splat of a bug on the windshield.

Eva dozed, head resting against my right shoulder. She must have been dreaming. I watched her nipples harden, jealous at the unknown source of her sleeping lust, and lit a Camel to keep from kissing her. Outside on the highway, the headlights shadowboxed with a few sparse trees. The clouds cross-hatched the stars. Inside Eva's bare and beautiful legs stretched beneath the dash. She rocked slightly to the rhythm of the road harmonizing with the low hum of rubber on asphalt and night folding over the green glow of the radio like a spent squeezebox. Janis Joplin ground out a gritty prophecy for my future in Mexico – *take another little piece of my heart, oh baby if it makes you feel good.*

In a couple of weeks this vacation would end and I would lose myself in the disjointed myth that life is something to be suffered through as I went back to a banal existence in rural Indiana. All the while, the real myth slept beside me, lips slightly parted. A loose strand of dark hair slipped across her silk cheek and I reached to brush it back, one last chance at one more trip…I brushed her breast instead. She stirred only slightly. Steering the truck, my hand grew numb, my mind barely conscious that while Eva loved boyish charm, it was only sweaty danger that excited her. I remembered Norman for an instant, the blind butcher from a former post-war oasis in Sugarloaf, New York, who used to levitate roast beef across a whirring electric blade with the power of a seer in his fingers. I wanted his magic. I wanted to stroke my friend Eva so gently that her own moaning woke her. I could have done it before the war and the chaos of Vietnam diffused my senses, making love an intellectual exercise too complex to simply squeeze and let go. In my mind I saw a vision of romance and tragedy, acceptance and rejection, a prophecy of love overwhelmed by the existential dread of an inability to live outside my imagination.

∗∗∗

"A self-fulfilling prophecy is an assumption or prediction that, purely as a result of having been made, causes the expected or predicted event to occur and thus confirms its own accuracy," or so noted Austrian psychologist Paul Watzlawick once wrote. I spent my Mexican vacation affirming his words, but not before roaring into Tucson to watch my friend Jim Hayes pretend to be a Navajo and hammer out some beautiful turquoise and silver jewelry on the work bench inside his tiny adobe hut.

"We sell these bracelets to the white man. It makes him feel less guilty for the genocide of our people."

"You're not an Indian, asshole." I said and opened an Olympia beer.

"I might be."

"And I *am* Jewish," said Joey. "So let's get real with that genocide talk."

"All I'm saying is that when you participate in the great peyote ritual your spirit comingles with the elders of the tribe."

"Is that what they call tripping in Arizona – commingling?"

Eva asked the question with that particular tone of voice indicating her bull shit alarm bell had just been triggered. She asked us to drive her over to see one of her best friends from high school who had recently married a drug dealer and moved to Arizona. Tucson had two things going for it in those days, dry warm desert air that suited Midwestern retirees and a close proximity to Nogales and the Mexican border. I understood why the dealer had moved from Indiana. He had a partner and a refrigerated truck and they made regular runs into Mexico returning with packages of frozen sea food from the port cities along the Mexican west coast. This "sea food" was then driven back to the middle of America, rolled in Zig Zag papers of varying flavors, and smoked at parties to exclamations between coughing fits that sounded something like, "Boy this Acapulco Gold is good shit" or "heavy, man, heavy." By the third time around a circle the conversation tenor got serious, "Being an astronaut is a good idea if only I was smarter," followed by "fuck being an astronaut, I am an idea" and the conversation stopper "who ate all the fucking Fritos?"

For the man I'll call Johnny, this line of work made perfect sense. He was dumb, fat, and cruel and looked exactly that way. A few years after our visit he found what he'd always sought, an early grave. What I couldn't fathom then and still can't after all my own unsuccessful relationships is the nature of attraction. His girlfriend, the one Eva came to visit, seemed intelligent and kind. She was definitely good looking, meaning she had nothing in common with Johnny. Almost any two people in the world can stand each other long enough to fuck, but once it's over what makes the days and weeks and months and years of misery worth the effort of staying together? I have never come to a satisfying conclusion on this matter and, as old as I am now, doubt that I ever will. Certainly those of us raised as Christians learned early on that we were unworthy of happiness until we died. Maybe, that's part of it, but it never seemed that simple to me. It's almost as if there's an overwhelming need for penance as a form of balance when in a sexual relationship because the sex feels too good. In my younger days that's how I defined love, the struggle between joy and guilt.

Headline – Alien life forms in the desert outside Tucson:

"Didn't I tell you?"

Hayes pointed over a slight rise and down into a ravine past some sage brush at the bank of a small creek almost devoid of water flow. Eva had remained in Tucson to reminisce high school over a few joints and a bottle of Boone's Farm apple wine with her friend. The desert beckoned. We answered the call.

"You did. You did," Joey said, removing his fogged up glasses and wiping his sweaty forehead with his tee shirt.

"Shut up, Joey, before you scare them away."

"Hell, McGarrah, they ain't rabbits. They know we're looking," Hayes said.

One of the most pleasant aspects of late winter in the Tucson desert revolved around the indigenous wildlife coming out from under winter cover and returning to its natural habitat. First of all, giant saguaro cacti bloomed with beautiful flowers and rearranged every image of the prickly plants in my mind created by cowboy movies. Then, desert scrubs swept the sandy floor fresh and clean. Rattlesnakes sunned themselves on rocks that seemed sculpted by Salvador Dali. Prairie dogs poked their heads furtively from burrows at random intervals, almost like I was playing one of those "pop-a-mole" games at a local arcade. Purple, orange, blue, and silver colored vegetation dotted the shadowed dunes with kaleidoscopic chaos and in alien shapes. Overhead a cloudless sky of pastel blue complimented the sun. Even the jungles of Southeast Asia could not compete with this environment for surrealistic beauty, especially when Hayes handed me the binoculars and I had a closer glimpse of the most magnificent creatures in the desert. Four young women sunbathed on blankets. They were topless and well-endowed with blossoming flowers of their own, or to quote Joey, "Look at all those beautiful tits."

"This is why I love you Joey," I said, "even though you're twenty-five your penis is still fifteen years old, just like ours."

Hayes smiled and jerked the binoculars from Joey's sweaty hands.

Headline – Bullfight on Asphalt:

Even emotionally regressed idiots having fun can talk about tits and drink Olympia beer for so long before they realize John Berryman was describing them – "life, friends, is boring..." but "Even to say so means you have no inner resources..." – in his famous poem. After two days of "bird watching" we kissed Hayes goodbye, corralled Eva, and pointed the truck toward Nogales and the Mexican border. We crossed without incident – it's much easier getting into third world drug-producing countries than getting out of them – and drove 250 miles along Highway 15 until reaching the port city of Guaymas in a jittery, cramped, exhausted bundle of flesh. Most of the anxiety came from driving in Mexico. I had forgotten since my last trip the trick to surviving Mexico's highway system, especially at night. You must remember, first and foremost, that every truck driver suffers from the illusion that he was meant to be a bullfighter.

From pickup to semi, each vehicle's cab gets wrapped in multi-colored Christmas tree lights and a statue of the driver's favorite saint straddles the dashboard. As you approach a curve on one of the narrow mountain switchbacks and meet an oncoming truck, like a bull you will be forced to make a decision because you will be challenged by a cape of flashing lights surrounding the specter of a bobble-headed religious icon. You must choose whether to remain *temeroso*, a timid bull unwilling to charge, or decide to perform an *acometida*, charging the truck swiftly. The truck driver will always strike a *desplante*, or a pose where he dares you to charge, and at some point on a narrow switchback three thousand mile from your home you will meet your *hora de verdad*, the moment of truth. If smart, you will be a *temeroso*, a timid bull that pulls to the shoulder of the road and waits for the truck driver to roar past, his *cojones* enlarged and yours shriveled to raisin size in your pants.

Headline – American Tourists Sodomized and Left for Dead:

I chose timidity for the most part until my irritated ego could no longer deal with compromise. We survived several close encounters, but the screams of Eva and Joey forced me finally into a sad little motel on the outskirts of Guaymas. We took refuge for the night in a room that could have been used on the Spanish version set of *Psycho*, paying our few pesos to a night clerk that faintly resembled Tony Perkins, in the dazed and crossed eyes at least. Nevertheless, a good night's sleep, huevos rancheros with chorizo and some café con leche revived us. Departing for Mazatlan in good spirits, we felt buoyed by a bright white sun in a cloudless blue sky. Nothing dampened our quest for adventure during the 700 mile trek along Highway 15, not even the roadblock. Yes, that's right. It seemed as if the highway system in Mexico required policing by little fat men in cowboy hats carrying WWII vintage Thompson sub machine guns. For our protection, they removed us from the truck, searched Eva's suitcase, particularly her underwear, for contraband, and after deciding we had nothing of value, let us drive on in exchange for a pair of sunglasses and a thousand pesos (about ten bucks in those days). Joey and Eva laughed. The episode seemed to them as a plot from a bad movie. On the other hand, I was relieved at the relative ease with which we escaped, having seen firsthand in Vietnam what could result from the combination of isolation, emotion, and weapons.

Headline – Tourists Rescued by Fun:

There are few things in the world more beautiful and calming to the spirit than the gentle ebb and flow of the Pacific Ocean at sunset, especially in Mazatlan, Mexico. At least, that's the way I felt as our dusty truck ran parallel to it. We found a clean, cheap hotel on the beach and settled in for a week parasailing, body surfing, sunbathing, fine dining, horseback riding, and general faux jet-setting activities that poor white trash from the U.S. could accomplish in Mexico where being wealthy meant holding a hundred dollars.

Joey and I prowled the savage back alleys of the port city late at night while Eva slept. We drank Pacifico beer and shot pool with greasy sailors off cargo ships in smoky bars barely lit well enough to see the cue ball. The drug dealers and dock workers wagered how much time would pass before one of us ended up sliced with a switchblade or clubbed with a pool stick. We smiled and lost our money with great dignity, which no doubt saved our lives. But, these kinds of common sense thoughts never crossed my mind in those days. I was Kerouac and Camus rolled into one, searching for the answers to questions that have none. Or, this was the romantic type of drivel I kept myself moving forward with and it was the danger that came from reading books like *On the Road* and *The Rebel* while trying to deal with memories of war.

Eva did her own daylight explorations, maybe hoping to find a Latin Jim Morrison among the hustlers and tourists along the white sand. Mostly, she seemed in a perpetual state of wonder as if we had brought her to a paradisiacal planet in some unknown and faraway galaxy. Whether we dined on fresh sea bass, sipped white wine, and danced in elegant restaurants, oiled each other as we tanned, or scoured the crowded marketplaces for rainbow colored scarves and hand carved soapstone chess sets, she laughed and played and grew emotionally from a reference point of honest innocence. Her face took on an expression of constant joy. I had never seen that kind of openness and freshness before. It came close to ruining my trip. Certainly, it turned me into a petulant child for a short time because I wanted something I could never have.

Headline – Cruel and Unusual Punishment for Immature Male:

I wanted to be falling in love. In many ways I already loved Eva and she seemed certainly worthy of my affection, but in those early post-Vietnam days what little emotional substance left to me after the war could be expressed only in generalities. Like discovering the location of a lion when it roars close the ground, emotion roared over me in diffused waves and paralyzed me with fear as I struggled to find its origin. Adoration, hate, anger, sadness, lust, joy all made the same loud sound in my psyche. They all felt like guilt. I discerned no nuance between love and lust and when Eva's sweet body aroused me in her tiny black bikini, rather than accept the feeling for what it was – desire – I chose to objectify it romantically to assuage my guilt for wanting anyone so sweet and young and innocent. I could only live with my constant inclination to run my tongue over her nipples and twirl it around her navel if I believed the feeling meant something deeper. I had no idea then, nor do I now, what *deeper* meant.

Neither did I understand at the time that the process, the journey, has always meant more to me than the end result. Like a shark must keep moving or die, I am a person who must keep moving toward some goal. I drive myself relentlessly toward something until I reach it and then immediately search for a new pursuit or find myself dying of an existential ennui. I would have hated myself if I had reached my goal in this case and become bored. At least now I recognize that a sexual conscience is as much a delusion on one end as "free" love is on the other.

Whatever the reasons for my confusion, the consequences remained internal. I never discussed them with Joey or acted out any amorous intent with Eva. We spent our time in Mexico as it was meant to be spent in those days, as adventure and exploration, as hedonism and visceral joy, as a way to not grow older or more responsible. I never told Eva the way I felt, either. Part of the reason lay with my inability to make myself vulnerable, a holdover character flaw developed in the killing fields of Vietnam. But a bigger part, I think came from my own lack of understanding about feelings, what they were, where they came from, what made some appropriate and others ridiculous flights of fancy.

Ultimately what I missed, and still do from time to time, is that fact that once you try to discern the way you're supposed to feel in a given situation and then create that emotion consciously, you're no longer really feeling anything. I know, I know, I know it's complicated being a fucked-up male full of ambivalent yearning and self-loathing. It's not necessarily the way we're made, but it is the way we most often end up making ourselves. I had a tremendous amount of good fun on this road trip as evidenced by the fact that I remember so much of it forty years later and still think fondly of Eva in that bikini from time to time.

On the other hand, as proof that good, Midwestern, Christianized men can never enjoy life without punishing themselves for their pleasure, I offer one last anecdote for your contemplation. The entire time in Mexico, I avoided the dreaded intestinal conflagration known as Montezuma's Revenge, the Gringo Gallup, or the Aztec Two-Step by drinking bottled water, eating peeled fruit, cooked vegetables, and well-done meat at expensive restaurants. I went so far as to gargle every day using cheap tequila as a prophylactic mouthwash. On our journey up from the bowels of Mexico, my bowels remained in perfect working order. Consequently, I had a voracious appetite, and so the little white truck stopped for snacks frequently.

As we approached the border near dusk, intending to drive through the night until we reached Jimmy Hayes and his jewelry shop in Tucson, we spotted a clean looking restaurant barely on the Mexican side. Our last meal in country was a feast and, for me, included a bottle of Sun Kist orange soda to wash down steak, corn, shrimp, peppers, refried beans and fried ice cream. Against any possible vestige of common sense, I decided such a clean, well-lit place so close to the American border would surely have sanitized water absent those tricky little bacteria that brought about the fecal waterfalls infecting so many less sophisticated tourists. I splurged and ordered a glass of ice to chill the tepid soda, and by the time we left Jimmy's two days later I traveled home seven pounds lighter.

The emptiness in my bowels became a metaphor for the emptiness in my soul upon our return. The vast majority of time since graduating from high school nine years previous had been spent exploring the rest of the world. Forced by a strange desire for normalcy after the war and a disastrous four years wandering the now failed counter-culture utopia, I returned to my home town and attempted a year working at the post office and being married. Both attempts failed miserably. Restless and stressed from a strained relationship with my parents, especially my father, I needed to be on the move again. On the other hand, I had to earn a living and maintain some external structure or go completely insane. Ironically, my father, my nemesis, my conscience, call him what you will, provided a solution.

Neither of us seemed conscious of what motivated him to

make the offer, or what allowed me to accept it. He has been dead fifteen years now and I think I finally may have figured that out. It's odd how the present can trap us in the past. Lately, all my dreams happen at 2:00 AM, the time he died. I wake on the edge of my own mortality with an image of some old argument proving nothing more than we were similar men who might have been friends if born in the same era, if wounded in the same wars. Instead, the world made us enemies that never quit loving each other.

Chapter Three

River Downs Race Track

 Alive with earthworms and chicken snakes and honeycombed with anthills, a small levee stood guard against the feral Ohio. It was built after the flood of 1937 when the bloated river had churned through Coney Island Amusement Park, the neighborhood homes around the race track, and finally shredded the barns on the backstretch like a giant combine come to harvest a whole season of dreams before they flowered. That was a long time ago, I thought, walking the uneven parking lot toward the levee, and people adapt or they don't survive.

 I had some slight experience breaking trail horses with a Mexican named Timmy while I lived in upstate New York after the Vietnam War and I remembered the excitement wrestling with those beasts had brought me. Escaping southwestern Indiana for parts unknown and for good seemed a wonderful idea. My father didn't mind my leaving either since it would reduce the stress we both felt from arguing constantly about my inability to live like "ordinary folk." A new thoroughbred horse owner, he had entered into the business as a tax shelter for some of the huge profits he was making as an automobile dealer in the early nineteen-seventies. He had been an inveterate gambler all of his adult life and buying racehorses with the hope of having a champion of his own was a gamble John Bill McGarrah couldn't resist.

He had agreed to send his three two-year-olds to River Downs Race Track in Cincinnati to be broken, schooled, and conditioned properly for racing by a young trainer and his wife who were just starting into business on their own with two caveats. The first was that they would be willing to turn the horses over to a more experienced trainer named Dan Wilson for racing at the proper time and the second that they would be willing to take me on and teach me how to care for race horses, an equine apprentice so to speak. In this way, my father thought I might learn enough to accompany his horses and work for Dan on one level. On another level, I'm sure he hoped hard work would keep me alive and put some boundaries on my wanderlust. At least he would have an idea where to find me.

Maybe it was the heat or the shirt hanging loosely over my lean frame, the elation of completing the drive to Cincinnati, or simply the joy of being young and powerful and still alive, that made me feel so light, free in a way I hadn't felt since playing baseball on the high school field a year before the war had thrust me into the company of hard and dangerous men and made me over as a hard and dangerous man. I teetered on the edge of a cliff, not one I might fall over, but rather one I had climbed. After my recent trip to Mexico, the plateau seemed within my grasp.

I was regaining the strength that comes from life having a purpose. All ideas and preconceived notions around that particular subject had been eviscerated by my participation in the Vietnam War. I came home from that war as a stranger, even to myself. Over the last six years since my return, I had slowly begun to realize that more than one person inhabited my soul, that living was a fluid process of many things coming together randomly and not a result of just being one thing or another. This discovery gave me a sense of anticipation in my new direction. The feeling opposed diametrically my state of mind only a few months before. The reality of not having the answer for every question, of not controlling every circumstance, terrified me less because I knew that horse people, like farmers, were given over to nature and her random acts, people who *expected* their lives to be beyond their control and relished that risk they took every day.

Everyone at this race track called River Downs lived subservient to the natural world and lived this way by choice. I had no awareness as to why an insight came to me now, only that the clarity brought me to this river behind this race track back gate simply to be alone for a few minutes before I joined my new employers at their barn. The June bugs rattled their wings. Grackles and gulls swooped over the trees and around the cut bank on the Ohio below.

The faint sounds of the life that was to become my own carried across the field of weeds and black asphalt of a cratered and cracked parking lot full of derelict cars and rusted out pickup trucks driven by the carnie-like backstretch population hard at work. Thoroughbreds whinnied. Tractors clanged and chugged. Grooms and hot walkers joked and drank beer while cleaning saddles, bridles, feed tubs, water buckets, and unpacking equipment for a new race meet in a new town. The tang of liniments and manure hung in the air for most of the way to the river, a burnt offering to the god of good luck. Maybe what I had never understood about the Vietnam War was the function of survival. Surviving wasn't a badge of shame to be squandered by a short life of self-destructive behavior. It was an honor. What I did with what I had been given either respected or disrespected those whose memories I carried onward.

I'm not referring here to some altruistic achievement or a Herculean task that might save the world. The simple act of going forward with a little hope, curiosity, and kindness was what my dead comrades expected in return for their sacrifice and where I had been failing for the last several years of my life. I had a chance here, an opportunity to master an esoteric trade that few people ever learned to do really well and I intended to make the most of it.

The race meet came to this small patch of the world on the Ohio-Kentucky border every May, a carnival of speed and animal electricity. All was as it should be in the camped enclosure behind me. In the air around me rose the stench of restoration from the water, decaying foliage and dead fish turning over to create new life. Silt and driftwood from unknown origins rushed by atop the current. Brown waves roiled and whitecaps swirled against their alien presence. The swollen liquid was hypnotic with its constant motion downstream into the Mississippi, into the ocean, and out beyond a vanishing point where the sun and water converged, where nothing and everything met.

Over my left shoulder, the ball of the yellow sun struggled into a salmon-colored sky toward dawn. My shadow stretched over the parking lot all the way to the tree line, large and animated, as if it had a life of its own. I had never thought about it before, but there can be no shadows without light. Chasing my shadow had brought me into the light. The scent of coffee and bacon riding on the smoke from a track kitchen just inside the guard shack at the back gate called me into its somnolent sanctuary where time had stopped long enough to replace a night's hard-earned sleep with the rowdy comfort of a hard day's work.

***

My new boss, the first actual licensed horse trainer I apprenticed with, the one who taught me the intricacies of running an old-fashioned hand-tied spider bandage across a horse's knee to allow circulation and flexing, the one who demanded I "bank" the stalls in the barn with fresh straw after a thorough cleaning like they did in "New York," and the one who instructed me on the delicate balance between grain and hay required for optimal nutrition, is a lawyer now. Perhaps his rigorous attention to details, his intellectual abilities, and his need for perfection in process rather than ever reaching a goal led him away from racing and into the pursuit of justice, or maybe he could afford better hookers on a lawyer's salary.

His wife, ex-now, coached me at trimming and braiding a mane and helped increase my riding skills (she was an excellent rider who later became a jockey), as well as showing me the proper way to clean a male horse's penis shaft. This last thing may seem rather perverse, but the fact of the matter is that, unlike dogs, humans and horses evolved beyond the necessary physical acumen to lick their own genitals. Is this a flaw in evolution? That may depend on your personal outlook. But if a stallion goes very long without having the dirt and dead skin removed from under his foreskin, he may experience tremendous discomfort and waddle rather than run around a race track. Like many human males, most stallions seemed more appreciative of this undertaking when left in the hands of a woman. I was bitten, kicked, butted, and stomped on more than one occasion. None of the horses seemed to even notice Sissy's presence beyond a satisfied nod of their massive heads.

Sissy left Barry when he became a fulltime and unrepentant adulterer while she was pregnant. After giving birth to a daughter, she revived her athleticism, "got fit" in race track terms and rode races for a few years to earn a living. She also became a drunk. His training business collapsed because his clients found other trainers who demanded less perfection from their training efforts and ran the horses more often with a view to earning money. That's when Barry entered law school. I hope they've both healed from the disease of knowing each other by now. I liked them very much and learned a lot about caring for race horses from them. Unfortunately, they had little to teach me about conditioning those horses and the over-all business of running a competitive public racing stable because they were afraid.

As with many people, including me, who can display physical courage when needed, they were afraid of life, sex, each other, lack of control, of having control, but mostly they seemed afraid to make a mistake. Consequently, they did nothing. Their horses became the healthiest at River Downs, but those same horses were never entered in a race against other horses. To Barry, they were never quite fit enough. They always needed just one more workout. The stable never had a chance to earn any purse money and it's the *chance* that keeps the owners of the horses you train coming back to you with other horses, as well as attracting new clients. The possibility of failure always accompanies the possibility of achievement. Business men who own race horses as hobbies and tax write-offs are well aware of this prospect. The equal opportunity for losing, however, made Barry and Sissy over-anxious about taking the risk of winning.

I don't know why they felt this way unless it was the fact both of them had led fairly privileged lives and were never really allowed to fail. Bottom line though, no sharp owner, no matter how wealthy, will pay tens of thousands of dollars for a thoroughbred and then pay thousands more each month to watch that same thoroughbred stand in a stall munching hay. The statement, "This horse is almost ready to run," can only be restated for so long before it's followed by this one – "Then, run the fucking thing." If only Sissy and Barry would have followed the example of the one old gelding they owned themselves, things might have ended differently. His name was Bam-Bam. Bam-Bam lost his balls as a two year old colt, but the memory of being a nasty, temperamental, vicious, stud remained locked deep within his tiny brain.

"Hey Jim, bring me the thermometer." Sissy yelled. I dropped the pitchfork in the next stall and walked to the medical box hanging on the barn wall. In a few seconds, I returned with a thermometer tied with a long string to a clothespin. Any break from picking up horse manure in a dark wooden stall on a steamy, fly-ridden August day brought me joy.

"You think the old Bam Bam's got a fever? He cleaned up his breakfast, didn't he?" I asked, handing her the glass device.

"I don't know. All of sudden he doesn't want to go to the track. He won't take the bit."

The bridle kept causing problems. As it went over the gelding's ears, Bam tried to back out of it. Sissy had her thumb and a finger on both ends of the bit against his clenched teeth. She wiggled her fingers, rubbing the gums and trying to tickle the mouth open. No good. The old boy had acted like he wanted to go to the track earlier, pawing at the stall floor and charging the webbing as he watched other horses train before him. What the hell was going on?

"Calm down Bam Bam. What's got you spooked old boy?" I said. "It's just another day."

Sissy tried again, then again. Both times the jaw was clamped tight. She was losing her patience. Her hands were trembling, possibly from a hangover. She shoved the bit hard against the horse's teeth. Bam threw his head and the whole bridle flew against the stall wall, falling into the straw, which was a common reaction by horses when something wasn't right. "Goddamn you, Bam. You're going take this bit and we're going to the track. I'm tired of fucking with you." Sweat poured off Sissy's forehead. She squinted and spit on the thermometer to moisten it and stuck it in the gelding's ass, clipping the clothespin to the tail so he wouldn't lose the thermometer in his bowels.

I appreciated the way Sissy's tight little ass fit into her jeans and how those jeans slid into a pair of leather riding chaps. I have great respect for works of art. But, most of all I admired her total disregard of the disgusting. She lacked squeamishness, a telltale girly trait that made it so very difficult for spoiled young ladies used to the dressage show horse circuit to break into the misogynistic barn yard environment of a race track backstretch. Sissy got sweaty and dirty and could curse with the best of us. On the other hand, she had impeccable manners and a Botticelli face and a disdain for crude sexual banter as any good Southern belle might. The conflict in her personality and her lack of availability drove my libido wild.

"He's got no fever. He's waiting for his pussy," Barry spoke as he entered Bam Bam's stall with us.

"He's a gelding, dear. He's got no balls, the same as you. What's he going to do with pussy?"

Oh, did I forget to mention Sissy's acerbic tongue, another of her personal qualities that often initiated my fantasies of sexual encounters with wild abandon on the army cot in the tack room where I slept at the end of the barn.

"Not that kind," Barry clucked. "He's waiting for the calico cat. Bam won't go to the track till he sees the cat and gets a chance to kick its brains out."

As usual, Barry had a point. He always spoke with great logic and precision, even when what he said made no sense. However, in this instance, I understood the connection. Every morning since this meet opened, a calico cat came by the stall, jumped on the outside ledge, and perched there till Bam Bam came out. And every morning, the old gelding walked three steps down the shed row, stopped and fired both back legs toward the furry ball, never coming close. The cat was much too fast to catch a hoof upside its head. No one knew where the cat came from, or who it belonged to. This could also be said about many of the men and women working at the track. But the cat helped me understand my new world in a better way. Race trackers were all superstitious, even educated ones like Barry. They connected their good or bad fortunes at a racing meet to some sort of material object that acted as a talisman. The connection for me seemed easy to make after Vietnam. If you had the luck of staying alive in Vietnam it got attributed to an object in your immediate sphere of existence, a charm of some kind that could be as simple as a Zippo or as complex as a snake-bone rattle made and blessed by a mambo priestess in some Louisiana voodoo cult. I deemed it perfectly normal for humans to require some kind of protection from random, inexplicable, unchangeable circumstance. For Barry and his small public racing stable, it was the everyday manifestation of a mystery cat and Bam Bam's playful attempt to murder it. This morning, the cat was late.

That was an omen and not a good one. I extracted the thermometer and held it up to the light, searching for the mercury.

"It's in the normal range, 100.2."

"Told ya. It's the cat." No sooner had he spoken than the

calico appeared and the horse whinnied, taking the bit into his mouth as if there had never been a problem.

As I unhooked the nylon webbing across the stall doorway that held the horse at bay, Sissy shook her head and led the big gelding out, walking him up a few steps. Bam made no effort to kick. The cat looked at him quizzically and stayed poised for the jump. "I'll be damn," said Barry as I took Sissy's left leg in hand, and gave her a "leg up" by hoisting her into the saddle. The gelding grunted unhappily as the rider settled into her seat. With her feet still out of the stirrups and me leading them around the barn, Sissy reached down and re-tightened the girth another notch. We all knew a horse's trick of holding his breath when first saddled, and if the girth wasn't tightened after he was forced to breathe, the saddle would probably loosen and slide off during the workout. Bam-Bam enjoyed games.

Moving around the barn, she put her feet into the stirrup irons, measured the straps to make sure the bend of her legs felt comfortable and then stood in the irons to insure their strength. When we turned the corner, reappearing on the front side of the barn, the calico cat waited as Sissy crossed the reins and knotted them to shorten their length.

"I wonder why he didn't try to nail the kitty this morning," Barry said, lifting his dirty ball cap with his left hand and scratching a prematurely balding spot on his head.

"Maybe he's giving it a rest. I'm ready. Wet this tongue tie and put it on," answered Sissy.

Handing me the strip of flannel cloth, she watched, holding the horse still as I dipped it in a water bucket, reached into Bam's mouth, pulled his massive tongue out sideways, wrapped the tie around it once, and then made a bow knot under the jaw.

"Make sure it's not too tight." Barry ordered.

I checked the tongue. Bam Bam could still wiggle it, but not get it over the snaffle bit and run off with his rider. "It's okay."

As usual for an anal-retentive person, Barry rechecked my work, twice, and snapped the leather shank on the D of the bit to lead horse and rider forward. I noticed a slight cock of the horse's head. Bam Bam appeared to measure the distance to the ledge as they passed by the second time. When they reached a position even with the cat, his back end jerked up and the cat got caught totally unaware. The force of a rear hoof fired it in the air and off the ledge. Tumbling end over end like a football, it landed in the muck pit on a pile of dirty, wet straw. The cat lay there for a minute, stunned.

"Jesus," said Barry. "I've never seen a cat land on its back before. It must be dead." With a frightened shudder, he handed me the lead shank on the horse and walked toward the senseless animal.

"Is it dead?" I asked.

He prodded it with the toe of his worn boot. The cat stirred and hissed. "No, the cat must've not caught the hooves at full extension. But it'll be crazy as a loon from now on, I bet."

"Why'd old Bam do that? I thought he and the cat were friends."

Leading horse and rider out of the barn toward the gap in the track railing, I directed my question at Barry.

"I don't know, but that was sure strange. I guess even friends aren't always trustworthy, or maybe the cat just got what it deserved for teasing him all meet."

"It's a sign," I said.

"You sound like an old hard boot race tracker already. Everyone I know is superstitious. They're also idiots. Watch out that you don't become an idiot."

I suppose two points might be illustrated by this memory of mine. First, it could be argued that the change in the cat's mental status brought about a change in fortune for the stable. On the other hand, changes can't really ever be quantified or qualified if you were doing nothing before and continue doing nothing after anyway. Inertia isn't related much to change. Barry never won a race after the cat episode. Depending on your basic knowledge of rhetoric, you could argue also that the cat's disappearance from the barn area after this day brought us bad luck. As a matter of fact, Barry always did argue from that angle. But, you could just as easily say that things remained the same because he never ran a horse after it.

The main lesson for me lay in Bam Bam's persistence. Goals may seem unreachable, but if you're willing to adapt your approach to those goals and keep trying, what was once out of reach may not be, really. I extended this line of thinking to the act of survival as a self-destructive, guilt-filled, war vet and it helped me move forward emotionally – not far, but forward nonetheless.

Chapter Four

Hard Boots

After a short, but valuable, apprenticeship with Barry and Sissy at
River Downs in Cincinnati, I went to work in 1975 for my father's
newest friend who had spent his life on various racetracks around the
country doing everything from cooling out thoroughbreds after
exercise as a boy, to riding races as a teenager, to grooming and
ultimately training said horses when he got too heavy to ride. This
earned him a label of affection and respect allowed to a lifetime race
tracker who worked at cheap, bush league tracks, drank hard, and
then worked harder seven days a week, and who considered his job a
way of life. Daniel Wilson was one of the last old-time "hard boots"
of Kentucky horse-country fame. It was true, he had risen above the
rank and file membership by showing initiative and talent to become
a trainer and operate his own business.

A public trainer was a man who developed clients as in any
business. Wealthy people looking for a fun way to hide their money
or spend it for tax credit sometimes bought thoroughbreds for racing
and to gamble on. This was the reason someone labeled racing "the
sport of kings." By the same token, this high-priced hobby could only
be conducted legally under the supervision and expertise of a licensed
trainer, a person who had passed a written exam expressing his or her
knowledge of horses and horse care and who had amassed
considerable on-the-job experience. As novices, horse owners often

selected a trainer at random, based on location, day rate, availability, or personality, rather than on actual ability, and then sent their property to that trainer to compete. Like most other things in a capitalistic society, horse racing functions on an economic hierarchy. Sometimes really talented people labored in obscurity because they got cheaper horses to work with, while idiots ended up wealthy and famous because they hustled a champion into their barn. A good horse can earn a living; a great horse can break the bank. The famous horseman Sonny Jim Fitzsimmons once quipped, "Trainers don't make horses, horses make trainers." The better class of races a stable won, the more money earned. Well bred, expensive animals competed at a higher level than lesser ones. That's what everything finally came down to.

My father, not rich in a real big-money sense, purchased relatively cheap, but solidly bred two year old thoroughbreds. They were unbroken and unraced. John Bill loved competition and he loved gambling, but he needed income from his automobile businesses to keep paying daily maintenance. Barry's slow insistence on perfection and subsequent refusal to run those horses gave them no chance of earning income back in races. This reality chased my father to Wilson's stable earlier than anticipated and me along with them as a condition of the transfer. Don't get me wrong, I had learned a considerable amount about caring for race horses in a short period of time. Not only were Barry and Sissy good teachers, but I became obsessed with taking in every aspect of track life from the moment I set foot on the backstretch at River Downs. I read veterinary textbooks, watched how the starting gate crew loaded horses, spoke with the Daily Racing Form's track reporter, questioned every trainer who would talk with me about his methods, followed the blacksmith around on my time off, and fell asleep checking breeding dosage and racing stats at night. Obsessive behavior has never been a problem for me. Once I start something it consumes me. Consequently, I was a pretty good stable hand with race horses when the three young ones belonging to my father were shipped out of River Downs to Dan Wilson.

Public racing stables like Dan's moved from track to track during certain days allotted by state racing commissions much like carnivals move from town to town on a circuit of county fairs each year. The term "public" simply meant that Dan accepted horses from random owners rather than being under contract to one big racing concern such as Calumet Farms or Meadow Stables. Management at each track supplied barns with individual stalls for the horses, a well-maintained dirt oval to exercise and race on, and prize money for which horses competed. The horse owners paid a daily rate to the trainer so he would athletically condition, feed, medicate, race, and in every way care for the horse. Theoretically, the daily rate covered a trainer's operating expenses, including paying salaries for the grooms and hot walkers and exercise riders who assisted him. Back in the seventies, my father paid twenty-five dollars a day per horse for three horses in training. Including his veterinary bill, he had around three thousand dollars a month going out of his pocket. Profit for everybody came from winning races and sharing the prize money. If a trainer was incompetent or had bad luck or was blessed with slow horses, life on the track got really difficult. It took tough men to weather the hard times and struggle with the cut throat competition in the days before huge corporations began taking over racing.

I would come to recognize the phrase "he's an old hard boot" as a term of respect and the men themselves as near mythical creatures whose lives were simultaneously elevated and destroyed by the myth. Every young person on the track wanted to be a hard boot. In some ways this was similar to the delusion thousands of white, suburbanite teenage boys would go through early in the 21st century claiming to be "gangstas" just like their favorite black rap stars. It all has to do with the romantic illusions of freedom and non-conformity conjured up by a particular culture. But just as middle-class white boys could never be African-American urban gangsters, so the title Hard Boot could never be earned by someone who entered the race track culture simply looking for a job and not a home.

Hard Boots were those men with single names like Monk, Hoss, and Red that made the racetrack a place of mystery. Because of them, the backside of every track took on its own special atmosphere. No one knew where they came from, or how long they had worked the horses. They were always there, traveling from one race meet to the next – Churchill Downs, Keeneland, Sportsman, Hawthorne, Fairgrounds, Oaklawn Park, and Ellis Park in the summer – always dodging the cold weather by a few weeks and the responsibilities of life by a few miles.

Horseracing was their birthright. Their mothers were the

nameless old women who cooked breakfast and made coffee at the track kitchens. Men that rose above the old hard boot character flaws of staying drunk and broke, men like Dan who seemed gifted with an almost savant type focus and singular genius, became trainers through hard work and talent and became surrogate fathers for them. Their brothers and sisters were those same thoroughbreds. They shifted from track to track in the horse vans. They slept on cots or feed sacks in tack rooms at the end of the barns in case one of the horses should colic, or get casted against the stall wall at night, and they wept when one of their families chipped a bone or bowed a tendon. Hard Boots had no unions and, except for the training stable where they worked, no relatives to speak of. They had a simple code of conduct – don't steal, don't lie, pay what you owe, and never mistreat a racehorse.

Joining the Daniel Wilson Public Racing Stable in the late summer at Ellis Park a new era of my life began. I was on a quest in search of a destiny, one that required little or no interaction with the banality of American society or the failed experiment called the counterculture. I had burned through the roles of athlete, soldier, student, social activist, and hippie in the first two decades of my life and now hoped to rise, a Phoenix, into the role of working professional. I had no idea what that role was, only that it required a certain structured and "normal" regimen and both qualities seemed important at this time in my life. However, all people carry their flaws with them because no matter how our lives get scratched and chipped, the scars are irrevocably imprinted in our character like the groves cut in a vinyl record. No matter what kind of a needle or what brand of stereo manipulates it, the song remains the same. Consequently, when I arrived at Ellis, my first reactions were boyhood memories and the outlining in my mind of what dusty old literary critics call a bildungsroman narrative that traces the psychological and moral development of a single protagonist from youth to adulthood. In other words, how the hell did I get to this point in my life and why had I bothered to come? Why wasn't I normal? What was normal? These were the questions that haunted me in the quiet hours of dawn after the dark had fled and before the sun arrived, the grey time when I rose from my army cot in the tack room to feed my charges a cup of oats for breakfast. Maybe this new environment at Ellis Park would answer them.

Outside the racing secretary's office I could smell straw, liniment, bad coffee, sweat, leather, and manure, all mingled in the air, even though I had yet to pass through the security gate and roam the backside. Actually the scent was rising from the group of trainers milling around the office door, coming and going, entering or scratching horses in various future races. It was a special morning odor and an everyday odor, full of anticipation and possibilities. It was the tang of life and like many other smells on the racetrack, it reminded me of my father and my first connection with the romanticism of horse racing. Those early days of childhood, of accompanying him to the track, had become the only thread of memory that held our relationship together for me. Except for this one common aspect rejuvenated now by my current job, we did not know each other.

Even though this was the "dark day" of the week when there no races were scheduled, I felt the ground vibrate as forty hooves drummed down the stretch. For an instant, the air seemed electric, swirling and crackling, like a jockey's whip had just sliced through it. The smell of leather and sweat rose everywhere in the air around me. I had that same feeling every time I walked into a race track grandstand and still do.

I had come to the office to be examined for a groom's license. I couldn't work on the backside of a racetrack for Daniel Wilson or any other trainer without a proper identification badge and my River Downs license carried with it privileges for the state of Ohio only. The barn areas of racetracks were secured areas. Why? Because horse racing involved huge sums of easy money and horses were valuable animals. Some method for limiting access to them by criminals and inept idiots had to be in place. Any business that promised easy cash from gambling has always been subject to the machinations of human greed. The powers that controlled this industry wanted to make sure that the money didn't get spread too thin, that it remained within the small circle of professionals who devised and operated the game. If you think that seems unusually restrictive in a free-market, capitalistic system, try getting on the floor of the New York Stock Exchange without a license.

Once I entered the room, Dan met me and led me through the procedure, signing his name in advance and thereby assuring security of his willingness to vouch for my character as it related to work with horses. Beyond that, Dan may have had trouble vouching for his own character. He was a man of medium height with a square face, his dark hair streaked with gray and his dimpled chin clean-shaven. He wore a beige leisure suit flecked with brown and red and a pair of silver-tipped cowboy boots that looked expensive, although I didn't know that they were necessarily. When Dan walked toward me, I noticed a slight list left, a limp he'd had since a tumble from a horse shattered his tibia bone two decades earlier. The bone was set incorrectly, probably by a vet rather than a doctor. His face was deeply tanned and wrinkled as if someone had wadded up a paper bag and then straightened the thing out over his skull. But, his blue eyes twinkled and he smiled incessantly, joking and bantering with everyone in the office as if they were all related. He smelled like a mixture of English Leather, horse hide, and vodka. What you saw was what you got – flawed personally, rough around the edges but direct speaking in his business dealings, and passionate about horses. Like many hard men, Dan was capable of great displays of spontaneous kindness, especially toward old drunks and animals. On the other hand, if called upon for sensitivity or intimacy in a personal relationship, he could and often did, respond with cruelty. I witnessed this narrow focus and simple understanding of how life worked on several occasions before I left his employ.

Once my fingerprints were recorded and my picture laminated on a badge, I walked to the end of the long grandstand area and climbed in my '67 Dodge pick-up truck. The incessant chatter from the office fused gradually into a slight hum like electric current in a transformer and then faded away beneath the hiss of my own tires over hot asphalt. Waved onward by the old man in a security guard's uniform, I drove slowly through the gate and down the backside of the racetrack past rows of barns like the one I'd just left. Every bush league track had the same country fair look, dirt footpaths running between a row of narrow barns that resembled freight cars abandoned on some Southern Railway siding, green shingled roofs extending out over low shed rows that circled the stalls beneath them, uneven wooden planks nailed at odd angles, hay racks and odd-sized tack boxes hung at various heights on walls that were peeling decades old paint. In a city, this kind of area would be called "the ghetto" and like that urban area, the poor congregated to survive whatever way possible.

Unlike an inner city, this was a happy place, a carnival of sweat and laughter. The humid and hot summer air bred hope and expectation rather than anger and despair. A band of gypsies lived here who were family and who were doing exactly what they wanted to do with their lives. The grooms raked shed rows, cleaned saddles and bridles dirt-caked from early morning use, and fed horses their late morning cup of oats. Some sat outside the barns on straw bales and smoked. There was no longer the dawn chaos. Everyone and everything had settled into a singularity of purpose and identity. I had those things once. Playing baseball in high school gave me those things. When I swung a good old Louisville slugger bat and made solid contact with some pitcher's best fastball, the electricity that ran through the wood ran through my body as well. I saw the world for what I wanted it to be, a Corvette Sting Ray with a turbo-charged engine and on most days, it felt like I was driving it. But that was almost a decade ago. A man can go through a lot of changes in ten years and my understanding of the simple brightness of life had grown dimmer during that time. My emotions had grown numb and my mind cluttered with half-thoughts, partial memories, refuse of survival. What had once been easily definable on a sunlit ball diamond now existed only as shadow. I wanted that rush of power that comes from feeling alive all over to return here at Ellis Park. And, I got my wish.

Chapter Five

Horsemen, Get Your Horses Ready for the First Race

The loudspeakers from the track PA system crackled. I followed Dan's directions and found myself sitting in the truck at the track kitchen, a white concrete block building that could just have easily been someone's garage. The sun shone directly overhead and my tee shirt was drenched with sweat. I drifted into a nap waiting for Dan to arrive.

"Goddamnit. Goddamnit. Listen to me. Give me a dollar for a beer boy."

A voice screamed from the world outside my mind. It sounded like a bird cawing.

"Goddamnit boy. Get out of the truck and give me a dollar."

"Shit, lower your voice. Who the fuck are you?"

A tiny man that resembled the crow he sounded like scratched his thin, crooked nose with his right hand and grabbed at his crotch with his left. I couldn't help but laugh at the bird-like movements.

"Well, then pay attention. Pay attention when I speak to you, boy, instead of staring off into space like you was getting some head or something. I'm Dan's messenger, like an angel come to give you the word. I say, I say I got connections too. You don't pay up, I get you booted off this track. Name's Wally."

"Where's Dan?"

"Why...he's inside waiting for your lazy ass like the rest of us. We don't get paid to sleep. No sir...no sir...we get paid for other things. Speaking of paid...you got that dollar?"

"It's yours if you shut up." I took a wadded bill from my pocket and shoved it at the dirty little man standing outside my truck. Panhandling was an honorable profession for drunks on the track. I took no offense at his request. The white stone on the restaurant front wall blinded me, as if a bare light bulb flicked on in a dark room or the knowledge of the universe unfolded from a single word.

"And, don't worry about my head, the one on my shoulders or the one in my pants. Worry about your own. I might just boot *you* off this track and kick you to the curb like the mangy dog you are."

"That's hilarious, for a retard. But, answer the question, why are you screaming at me? I AIN'T DEAF, BOY. Dan's inside drinking his lunch and he requests the presence of your majesty AT HIS TABLE."

The man called Wally grabbed the money and ran back into the track kitchen ahead of me. Smells of sausage and bacon grease, toasted bread, and coffee brewing reminded me of my hunger. My pulse quickened, whether from the smell of food or the expectation of sitting down and getting acquainted with my new boss Dan, I didn't know. I ordered two eggs over easy, bacon, and an English muffin from the woman behind the counter who looked exactly like a frumpy lunch lady from any junior high school cafeteria in America. She drew a cup of black coffee from the stainless steel machine, handed it to me, and I walked towards the table.

The kitchen looked the same on this day as it did most late mornings on every race track I ever worked during the next several years. The tables along the west wall were crowded with grooms and hot walkers arguing over who had the best horse in the best stable, drinking beer, laughing too loudly, and throwing their hands in different directions to punctuate their words. Occasionally, one of the braver girls would venture an opinion and then promptly be ridiculed for having no balls, and therefore no intellect. Women were still an oddity on the backside of mid-western race tracks in the 1970's and most of the men viewed them as an inferior species of beast to be used when expedient and disregarded at all other times, like the dogs that guarded the feed sheds.

I thought the bias a very stupid and costly one. The women I knew rode better than me, especially Sissy. They were neater around the barn, gentler and cleaner with the horses, certainly more reliable workers. Most importantly, if you have to spend all morning looking at a groom bent over a horse in the barn, why should it be an ugly man? This attitude made me feel enlightened and probably came as close to reconciling with the feminist movement as I could muster at the time considering my abject failures in past relationships with the opposite sex and my lifelong indoctrination into the cult of over-masculinity.

Exercise riders sat at the tables in the center of the room. If the racetrack was a closed caste system, riders would rank above grooms, who ranked above hot walkers. The trainers would occupy the highest caste because they paid the bills and gave everyone else employment. The jockeys, who ranked between trainers and exercise riders but considered themselves the highest caste because their jobs were the most dangerous, had already left the kitchen and reported to the jock's room, a small hut next to the paddock where the horses were saddled for each race. Kentucky racing law required them to be out of contact with everyone except their valets and each other during the racing program every day. The reason for this was to keep them honest in the inherently dishonest business of gambling that made the sport of racing possible. It sounded like good strategy, but any tricks or fixes, which were rare, had been arranged long before post time. I have come to understand over the last few decades that compared to politics, the sport of horse racing is honest. And, as far as the hierarchy crap went, every racetracker from hot walker to jockey to groom or trainer was one hundred percent positive every time a horse won a race that his effort with said horse had been the reason why. Each job provided a symbiotic relationship for every other one.

At the four or five tables along the east wall a few trainers who had no horses running that afternoon played euchre with a worn deck of cards and discussed the day's racing program or a cocktail waitress they had tried to hustle the night before. In an hour, the whole kitchen area would be deserted. The trainers that had no horses running on the day's card would go to the grandstand on the front side of the track and watch the program. The dumb ones would gamble, thinking they possessed some mystical insight into the order of finish in each race. Some exercise riders would tack their ponies and earn extra money, leading the thoroughbreds to the starting gate. The grooms and hot walkers would return to their barns, drink beer, and nap till the time came to mix the evening feed. It was the rhythm of life on the racetrack. Its simplicity and consistency kept me in a groove that required only the basic animal instincts to survive and left my mind free to wander randomly, an activity my mind needed desperately at this time in my life.

"I see the boss man has opened his table to peons," Wally said, nodding to a scraggly looking crew of stable hands. "Does that mean I can sit down too?"

"Hell no. You sit your ass on a hay bale and drink beer all day anyway," answered a heavy set woman. "What you want to bother real people like us?"

"If you're real, then life is a nightmare, you tub of lard," Dan spoke to the woman with a beer can on the way to his lips. "Let me buy you a PBR, Mr. Jim McGarrah. Monty and I were just talking about putting new shoes on a two-year-old colt. I'd like to breeze him tomorrow out of the gate with stickers on the back. The track's going to be a hard pull the next few days. Dean's got the damn track harrowed so fucking deep and it's so full of sand, the horse needs some extra traction. It's like running on a beach for god's sake. I know you can ride a little and I know you can groom a horse, but can you hold a nasty little colt still for the blacksmith. What do you think?"

"I think I can handle the task."

"Just don't trim him too close, Monty," said Dan as I sat down.

"You ever know me to trim a horse too close?"

"Depends on whether or not your wife makes you mad the night before."

"She don't make me mad anymore. She knows who the boss is."

"And she knows it sure the fuck ain't you," the woman slurred her words.

A man everyone called Barrel laughed loudly. He was huge, at least three hundred pounds of flab and stink and diabetic with a tiny head that included bulging frog eyes. As a matter of fact, when I glanced at him from the corner of his eye, Barrel even looked green and puff-cheeked like one.

"It's a good thing you know a lot about horses because you smell like piss and skunked beer." Monty smiled at the woman when she spoke. An outsider would have felt uncomfortable at the constant sniping, but on the track this flinging of insults back and forth was a way to share friendship, to be intimate emotionally without being intimate emotionally.

The banter here differed very little in form and substance from routine conversations in fraternity houses or in the Marine Corps, both places where I had spent considerable time. In today's politically correct world, a man can be fired and sued for speaking in this manner, especially if females are present. It's called "creating a hostile work environment." Evidently, some humans have only recently discovered that work environments are all pretty much hostile by nature. I guess being unfamiliar with the copper mines in Chile, the migratory farms in California, or the child armies in Africa, have led these people to believe a work place is hostile because *words* are sometimes offensive. Evidently the old proverb "stick and stones may break my bones, but words will never hurt me" itself is very painful in a polite society like ours (sarcasm intended here if you're too politically correct to detect it).

"You guys all think we live and breathe to keep you happy." The heavy woman with broad shoulders, dark, closely cropped hair and a masculine dimpled jaw spoke slowly. Her voice, which sounded like a pre-pubescent child's, didn't match her appearance.

"I know you could make me happy right now, Jade. If I wasn't afraid your lover boy Dan would fire me, we'd be rolling in the hay." Wally upended and drained his beer the moment the last word cleared his lips. Handing Barrel the dollar bill purloined from me, he nodded toward the counter. "Get one for the new boy. too, and bring me the change. I've already bought you three cans this morning."

"Won't be no change, you prick." Barrel grunted as he rose.

"You don't need to worry about rolling in the hay with me, old man. The way you drink, you getting into me would be like sticking a wet noodle up a tiger's ass."

"You got me there." Wally grabbed the money from the table top before Barrel could and walked to the counter. I looked into Dan's eyes. They were already beginning to glaze over, as were the eyes of two tiny Hispanic males at the table. Neither of these men had spoken a word. Later that afternoon, I found out that they worked for Dan and spoke no English. He communicated with an elaborate set of hand signals and a few words of Spanish what he expected from them. They complied without question and always. I would learn very quickly that this was the daily routine – drink beer beginning immediately after the morning work finished till post time, go to the races, drink vodka all afternoon while watching the horses run and swap tall tales with other trainers, the stories growing wilder as the day wore on. In many areas of life that would make my new boss a dysfunctional alcoholic. But, Dan would walk away from the bar when the racing program was over and know the horse that won each race, the equipment they wore, the way they pulled up after, and whether or not buying them would be a good investment for his clients. He would go home, fall asleep by dark, and be back at the barn by 5AM the next morning checking his charges and devising the morning's training schedule. Dan would do these things seven days a week without complaint and with a considerable amount of talent. For this ability, I soon regarded him with respect, if not awe.

"I guess you figured out by now that this is my pony girl, Jade. She takes the horses to the post in the afternoon and helps out around the barn."

"That ain't all I do, Sugar."

Wally returned with beers and my breakfast. Monty lit a cigarette and Jade asked me playfully, "You going to drink Pabst Blue Ribbon with eggs and bacon?"

"Why don't you and Jim have a little racetrack marriage, then you'd know what he eats and drinks all the time? He's younger than this beat up old trainer you're shacking up with now." The smoke from his lungs punctuated Monty's words. Jade gave him a dirty look, which appeared more menacing because her blue eyes were slightly off center on an otherwise perfectly square face. She stood.

"I've had a racetrack marriage or two and if I wanted another one, you can be damn sure I wouldn't ask you to pick my partner. Besides, me and Dan is in love, ain't we sweetheart." She blushed, her cheeks turning bright red instantly. Monty must have struck some kind of nerve and that was saying something. That very afternoon, I watched her on her Appaloosa pony leading a race horse to the starting gate. The colt was skittish and rank. It reared and then backed up, pulling her out of the saddle and over the top of the pony's neck and head. She did a somersault in mid-air and landed on her feet without ever dropping the lead shank, a considerable feat for a bowling ball with legs.

"Goddamn woman, shut that kind of talk up or I'll run you back to the quarter horse circuit where I found you."

She turned and walked out the door without saying goodbye to anyone.

"Thanks for running off the old ball and chain. She'll be whining for me to tell her I love her all afternoon." Dan finished his beer and smacked Monty across his arm.

"How'd I know she was so sensitive?"

"Who said she's sensitive? No woman likes to be called a whore."

"I didn't call her a whore."

"A racetrack marriage is nothing more than a one night stand that turns into two nights. Women don't think like we do. Hell, you're married. You should know that."

"Yeah, but my wife don't seem to think at all."

"That's obvious by her choice of husbands," Dan said. "Enough bullshit. Jim, set up a time with Monty and hold that young stud colt while he does the shoe work. Oh, and then don't forget to pack the feet with mud when he's done. I want to pull out any heat from the trimming. If that horse gets a sore foot, I'll strangle both of you. I'm going to the races."

"Yeah, I'm going to the races. I'm going to the races," said Wally. "I'll see you there, boss."

"I'm not giving you anymore money, you little shit. Don't bother me over there."

"Yeah," Monty said. "If you get too close to Dan, people might see the resemblance and think you was brothers. Especially if they knew you was both from Kentucky and your parents could be first cousins."

Dan stood and flipped his middle finger up under Monty's chin. "Just shoe my horse right asshole. No foot, no horse."

"No horse, no need for ugly blacksmiths," said Wally.

The four stable hands followed Dan out the door like lost children, three stumbled while the other one waddled.

No conversation like this would ever have occurred with Sissy and Barry at River Downs. Both of them were college educated and developed their love of horses in the show ring. Their parents supplied them with horses, dressage lessons, and a convoluted façade of genteel southern manners. Yet, the bond between the calloused Dan and the roughhewn, plain-looking Jade proved stronger in the long run than Sissy's and Barry's marriage. Also, I was beginning to discover that even in the same small neighborhoods, neighbors were often very different from each other.

Chapter Six

The Artist

Monty lifted his tools from the bed of the truck and tied his leather apron around the waist while I pulled a skittish two-year-old colt from the stall and centered him in the shed row. I rubbed Kentucky Honey's nose gently, whispering in his ear, attempting to calm any fear the blacksmith's presence generated. It wasn't that getting new shoes hurt the horse; it was just the idea that something would upset his day. Horses behaved like people in that respect. Everything living created its own comfort zone. Inside that zone, the world stayed quiet. Outside, chaos reigned. The object for most animals – remain in the comfort zone as much as possible and argue with anyone or thing that attempted to drag you out of it. Where we, as a society, have failed in my lifetime with our young men and women is by making war part of our comfort zone. We are a nation at peace with the prospect of war. Consequently, we no longer argue as politicians drag our young from their comfortable lives and place them in life or death situations for the economic and personal agendas of multi-national corporations. This tragedy was not clearly understood by me for many years. I knew vaguely that something had been done to me and I didn't feel quite right in the head but had no conscious awareness of how or why.

Monty set a wooden toolbox in the dirt and took a pair of clippers from it. He lifted the left front leg, rested the hoof on his knee, and began clipping the heads off the horseshoe nails. I jiggled the shank chain across Honey's nose, keeping his attention. After the nails were clipped, the blacksmith opened the clippers, gripped the shoe, and pulled it from the hoof. He traded the tool for a heavy metal file and, with a precise stroke, filed the overgrown hoof down flat. As he worked with his back to me, his words seemed to roll around his head and hang in the heavy air. I tried to see them as if they were in a circle of white paper above some cartoon figure in the comic section of the newspaper. If I saw the language, then the meaning couldn't hide. My mind had to work most days to focus on the present. Without concentrating, I seemed to slip into the past and my thoughts whirled dervish-like around a frenetic string of memories devoid of positive substance. They contained body parts, explosions, marriages, bad acid trips, fear and loathing that would make Hunter Thompson cringe. Those images felt bad enough, but at times I would seem to focus on a specific point and languish for long periods as if I were watching a movie, a replay of childhood that starred someone who was me but not really me.

"So you just started working for old Dan?" Monty asked.

"Yeah. I was doing some grooming at River Downs. But, my old man owns three of these horses Dan's got and I figured to learn as much as I could about training horses, which wasn't happening where I was."

"Well Dan's a good one to learn from. He's a lot better judge of horse flesh than he is women. You'll see that quick enough if you hang around Jade. She ain't bred for no stakes races. She's definitely a claimer."

Monty pulled a new aluminum shoe from a box of four, measured it against the horse's hoof, placed it on his portable anvil, and adjusted the size of the soft metal by banging it with a small hammer. My job of holding the horse could have been done by a post stuck in the ground. Bored and restless, I wanted Monty to work faster. The faster the work went the less time wasted. The less time wasted, the more I lived with a sense of accomplishing something. Since the war, I felt guilty when doing nothing. A man who survived on borrowed time, a man who should have died in combat only has so much time left to get things done. It made no difference what those things were. I just wanted to feel as if my life had been spared for some reason, some purpose slightly beyond my grasp at this point in time. It eased the guilt for having been spared at all. That need, among others, drove me to the race track in the first place. I was doing nothing in Princeton, Indiana, when I left. I had done nothing in college before that.

"Hey, pull ole Kentucky Honey up a step or two so I can work in the shade. It's fucking one hundred and three here today," said Monty.

I complied and then brushed away a fly from the white patch on the colt's forehead. The air had grown so thick and humid, even this normally aggressive animal languished in a hypnotic reverie. The hum of the fans, the heat, and the familiar voices rocked the horse to sleep gently and it paid no attention to the clang and rattle as Monty worked on. Wally and Barrel were surely at the paddock bar begging Dan, or anyone else that might listen, for drinks. The afternoon race card would soon begin. People from the area came to bet every day.

When the first shoe had been measured and corrected, Monty held it in place and drove small nails through the shoe around the rim of the hoof quickly and perfectly. Releasing the horse's leg, he moved to the left rear and started the procedure all over. Watching him work I began to realize that art wasn't a label that could be attached to old paintings. Art was work done uniquely and well. As a matter of fact, I had read once that the word originally meant to join things together with skill, exactly what a good blacksmith does by fitting a shoe to a hoof. An artist was a person whose work defined his soul, a person whose skill formed a way of life beyond the term job. Whenever people spoke of Monty, they called him the blacksmith, not the tall man or the blond one, or the guy who was kind to dogs and women. His art was inseparable from his identity.

I remembered Joe Whitehouse, the man that worked at my father's auto dealership when I was a child, the man who wanted to be a painter and became the best auto mechanic I ever knew. I felt a little homesick for an instant. Observing the grace and passion in Monty's movements, I hoped he would never have to reach the crossroads Joe Whitehouse did. When you abandon your art, you abandon your very self.

***

The perfume of spilled motor oil soaked in sawdust, along with carburetor jets dipped in grease-cutting solvent rose around me as I dribbled a new official Wilson leather basketball.

I had celebrated my eleventh birthday and confessed to my father that, when I grew up, I wanted to work as an automobile mechanic. My father, who knew me very well, realized I had a brain given to abstract problem solving and day dreaming, while my abilities with practical matters and hand-held tools lay somewhere beyond my ability to fly. "You could tear up a fucking anvil with a wrench," he claimed on his gin-drinking days. Consequently, he hung a basketball goal from the rafters in the huge shop area of his successful Dodge dealership. In these back bays, mechanics labored over warranty claims and oil changes while I shot free throws.

My father's plan performed brilliantly, and I was distracted enough through the early nineteen-sixties to make the high school basketball team and go on to college rather than toil away with a closet full of grease-stained clothes and fingernails that never came clean. But it wasn't so much the idea that sports trumped auto mechanics as it was the realization that I could never do what Joe Whitehouse did the way he did it. This is the lesson I learned on the particular Saturday in January when I received my new basketball and dribbled it while Joe prepared to tune up a Dodge Coronet with a 318 cubic inch engine.

First, he poured a mound of Velvet tobacco onto a small white paper as thin as a new blister. He licked the glued paper and lit the cigarette with a wooden match, striking it against the concrete floor as he knelt to contemplate the morass of sick metal before him. I quit dribbling, tucked the ball under my arm and approached the car.

"Hand me that wrench, boy," Joe said and stood, uncoiling his six-foot-four-inch frame until he towered above me. At first, I thought of my mother's favorite fable, Jack in the Beanstalk, granting Joe giant status. But as I look back on the scene now, I realize he more closely resembled the stalk with a huge flat head flowering from his calyx of a neck. Blue smoke spiraled from the cigarette between his lips. "Goddamnit, where's my wrench?"

I looked at the open drawer of his red Snap-On tool box only to find a cluster of various sized, shiny wrenches. I had no idea which one he wanted, and I was afraid to ask.

"You deaf, boy?" he roared.

"Which one, Joe?"

"Huh. Good question." His voice softened as he removed the cigarette from his mouth and flicked a long ash onto the floor. "Let's start with a 9/16th."

Having no idea what the numbers meant, I tore through the drawer, rattling and clanging wrenches till I saw the magic numbers on one. Placing the cold metal in his palm, I watched in awe as it, and the other tools he used over the course of that morning, came alive. The engine, trembling beneath his soft touch, spread itself open and exposed the mystic properties of its internal combustion soul. I had never witnessed a thing this remarkable. I had seen puppies born, rain fall with the sun shining, movies appear in a square wooden box my father brought home from the appliance store, but never a whole engine come undone into so many seemingly unrelated pieces, and so quickly. Joe seemed to know what tool he needed and what it was needed for by instinct alone. He never faltered, never hesitated, and never quit till, like a jigsaw puzzle shaken and poured from a box, bolts, nuts, plugs, gaskets, bearings, plates, relays, and wires lay strewn across the metal tabletop behind him in no particular order. How could anyone return it to its original majesty? More than that, how could it become greater than the sum of these insignificant parts and work right again?

"Was your dad a real Indian, Joe?"

"Cherokee. I ain't as lucky as you."

"What do you mean?"

"I mean, he gave me a love for expensive cars and cheap whiskey, and that's all he ever done for me. Your dad does a lot more for you. Hell, I ain't never had a basketball."

"My dad can't fix a car."

"No, he can't. He don't know the first thing about fixing cars, but he sure can sell 'em. See, every man can do at least one thing real good with his mind, and every man can do at least one thing good with his hands. But if that one thing is the same thing, and he puts his whole heart into it, then he maybe gets to be an artist at it. For me, it was fixing these hunks of metal. For your dad, it was baseball. Problem is, after he come home from the Second World War, he didn't have his heart in sports no more. But that don't mean you get to disrespect him 'cause he put his heart into making a living for his family and raising you kids right." Joe set the wrench on the fender and leaned back against the metal table to roll another smoke.

I'd like to say that Joe's words elevated my admiration for my dad and I carried that respect through adolescence. However, truth be told, I had begun to enter that phase of life where sons recognize the flaws of their fathers.

At noon, my father barked over the intercom and ordered me out of the shop area and into his office at the back of the showroom floor. It was lunch time. Joe kept cleaning parts and lubricating various fittings while dad and I drove two blocks up Prince Street to Dick Clark's Drive-In and bought a bag full of DC burgers and chocolate shakes. I ate mine as we drove back to the dealership. I wanted another, but didn't ask because I knew they were for Joe and the rest of the crew.

While the mechanics ate their burgers, Dad and I spoke briefly about how to focus on shooting free throws. I sat in his office, and he spoke across the huge desk as if I were a customer buying a new Dodge.

"When you're in the middle of a game, any game, you can't let the crowd distract you. You can't let the other players distract you. You have to shut out everything but the task at hand. You can't hear the noise or see the cheerleaders. Put a letter or a number in your mind. When I pitched, I always used the number 8. I put it right in the middle of the catcher's mitt. You need to put it right over the rim of the basket and then hit it with the ball. Except for the number 8, your mind should be totally blank."

Sports seemed to be the only topic he was willing to cover. Whether he thought it was the only thing I needed to know at eleven years old or whether it was the only subject he felt safe talking about, I never figured out until I spent a year in Vietnam and learned about the fear of intimacy and the other strange emotions that burden combat survivors for the rest of their lives. I just listened and returned to the shop area to practice his advice. At one point during the afternoon as Joe reassembled the engine, I hit thirty-seven consecutive free throws. I might have gone on infinitely, but then Joe started the engine he had been overhauling. The starter whirred just as the ball left my fingers. I missed, distracted by the odd sound, and hung my head in shame. I had lost my focus. Had my father been there to see it happen, he would have shaken his head and granted me failure status. The remarkable thirty-seven free throws hit beforehand would simply have been what he expected from his son.

"Missed one, did ya boy?" said Joe.

"The noise...,"

"Yeah, the starter solenoid's got a burr on it. It'll go out one of these days, but not today. My work order here says fix the engine, and that's what I did."

"I made over thirty shots before I missed one."

"What would your dad say?" Joe smiled, baring a wide row of caramel colored teeth, and rolling another cigarette.

"He'd say 'If you were half as good as you thought you were, you'd be twice as good as you are,' and then he'd tell me to remember what I did wrong when I missed."

"That's 'cause we learn from our mistakes."

"That's because he wants me to be perfect."

"No, he don't want you to be perfect. He just knows the world's a tough place and he wants you to be better than him so it don't weigh you down so much."

All the time we were talking, Joe leaned over the car fender and cocked his head in toward the engine, which idled so smoothly it seemed to be turned off.

"Hear that?"

I confessed to hearing nothing. Joe told me to close my eyes, and then he walked me into the car, lifting me and setting me like a bag of groceries on the fender.

"Now what do you hear?"

Putting the number 8 in my mind as if I were on the free throw line, I focused on the smooth hum of the cylinders, the rods, the lifters, and the bearings. They all worked in perfect unison so that the engine sound seemed part of the natural world, indistinct from everything around it.

"Nothing," I said.

"Keep your eyes closed and just listen to the engine, nothing else."

Somewhere deep within the bowels of its metal body, a slight ticking sound clicked against the even hum of everything else.

"I hear it, Joe. It sounds like a cricket."

He laughed and reached behind him into the red toolbox. Taking a long screwdriver from a drawer, Joe leaned into the engine and adjusted a tiny screw somewhere underneath the carburetor. The tick disappeared, and I witnessed the creation of something perfect, something that had grown as a whole to have a life of its own way beyond the simple re-ordering of its parts.

Not long after that day, on another Saturday afternoon when the shop had been shut down for the weekend, Dad gathered all the salesmen, bookkeepers, mechanics, and me together for a good-bye party in Joe's honor. The tall Cherokee had taken the job as chief mechanic in the local coal mine fixing the big draglines and motors that mined the coal. The pay scale and retirement were way beyond my father's means. Even though Joe's first love was automobiles, he needed the job for his family's sake. It was the right thing for him to do. Joe knew it, and my father accepted it gracefully. I remember the party well because it was the last time I saw Joe. Within a few short years, his heart exploded. The whiskey he drank and the cigarettes he constantly smoked got all the blame, but I never accepted that diagnosis.

At the party, Joe sipped my father's Canadian Club from a paper cup and told me about a newspaper article he had read that very morning. It concerned a man in Louisville, Kentucky, who went to sleep one night and awoke the next morning speaking French, a language he had never heard. The story said there were only twelve cases of this phenomenon ever reported in the world. But Joe focused on the man's words rather than the miracle of the man's new language: "Je suis perdu et seul," which translated means I am lost and alone.

"This is what happens when people have to live in one life while they belong in another," Joe said. Then he told me of a vision he'd had once as a young boy. His father had taken him to an old fashioned sweat lodge on a reservation out West someplace and during the ritual of cleansing Joe went through, a dream came to him. In the dream, he painted winter wheat as it roiled and bubbled, trees at the moment they became forests, dawn as it drained starlight from lakes, and autumn as it spun leaves into kaleidoscopes of color.

"I put that dream into my life with a set of tools instead of brushes," Joe said. "My canvas has always been an engine block, and I've always been happy. Now I'm gonna work on huge monster machines, chunks of metal with no feeling and no finesse just to make more money. I hope I don't end up like the guy from Louisville who can't remember who he is or where he's from."

***

"I heard you was some kind of war hero. That true?" Monty asked, while pulling a rear shoe.

"I was in the war. That doesn't make me a hero."

"You kill a lot of people in Vietnam?"

"Did you?"

"Didn't go. I'm from Kentucky. People from Kentucky are too smart to fight over anything but a racehorse or a woman. That make you mad?"

"Because you're from Kentucky?"

"Because I didn't go."

"Not particularly. Nothing makes me feel too much of anything anymore. I am curious how you beat the draft, though. You look to be prime age for cannon fodder."

"Got one leg shorter than the other. Us Kentucky boys always got an angle."

Chapter Seven

Us Kentucky Boys Always Got an Angle

Monty straightened up and stretched his back, then took the small, white towel from his toolbox and wiped the sweat from around his eyes again. I knocked slow moving flies away from Kentucky Honey's ears and gently patted his neck to keep him quiet. The colt was beginning to squirm and stomp a little, his patience wearing thin with the constant chafing of monotony.

"You're a lucky man. Not everybody from Kentucky stayed out of the draft and now I'm finished talking about the war."

"Okay by me. Didn't mean to step on any toes. It don't mean shit here on the racetrack anyway."

Monty finished shoeing the left rear and moved to right front. I could feel myself drifting, again. The heat, the inertia, the triggering conversation, all of it held me in a stupor. At first, I fought the pull like a swimmer might struggle against an undertow, stroking and kicking toward the present, but the past running beneath the surface dragged me under and drowned me.

This struggle seems to be difficult for people who have lived relatively sedate lives to understand. You can never change the past, but you can't forget it either because it changes you. Any person who has suffered through in-your-face combat must deal with intrusive thoughts. They may be random and appear unrelated. They seem to rise from nowhere and trail off without warning. Intrusive thoughts--

a clinical term thought up by a shrink trying to figure out why Vietnam vets were coming home so dysfunctional and unable to reintegrate into society. Finally, someone figured out after a lot of psychotherapy that the reason we found ourselves unable to adjust to being home was because we never really came back. A combat veteran lives in two worlds simultaneously, the present and the past. His outer reality is never quite balanced with the inner one, which is full of memories that keep popping up uninvited as if the subconscious were one of those jack-in-the-box toys. A word, an image, a smell, almost anything can wind it up till it springs out all over the conscious mind uncontrolled and often terrifying or incredibly sad. If you're having a really good day and if you're lucky, it may be pleasant like my memories of Joe Whitehouse. But, since pleasant memories of war are rare, the odds are stacked against them remaining pleasant very long. I believe personally that it's the new you chasing around your mind in a search for the old you. If you finds you, then YOU won't feel so lost.

The thing clawing its way out of your repressed thoughts may be disconnected shadows – faces of the dead, body parts, an explosion, a wilted flower, a broken banyan tree, a necklace, a gold tooth, a pack of smokes, a crying child – to any specific narrative you remember, or it may be a complete scene unfolding on the edge of a scream, especially if you can't remember the ending. When the mind fills with these intrusive pictures present tense actions risk being influenced, maybe even dominated, by past actions. *You* never come home from war.

I was enjoying my movie-like trip back to Joe and my father's garage. But, once the blacksmith mentioned being from Kentucky and evading the draft, I kept seeing Maynard's face. Maynard was a mechanic like Joe and a man like Monty, a man with an angle, a good old boy from Hazard, Kentucky. He and I were thrown together in a cavernous warehouse full of medical equipment and strangers in white coats, the induction center in downtown Louisville.

My stomach fell through my ass with fear when I walked in that door. An ugly man with a pock marked face and black-rimmed glasses, whose only name seemed to be Corporal, screamed and pushed me from one line to another. By 11am, Jim McGarrah had been measured, injected, poked in every orifice, prodded, and finally forced to cough as a pale doctor stroked my balls, looking for someone referred to as "Mr. Little Hernia." After lingering lovingly on his knees, the doctor rose and told me to pull up my shorts. I thought it was over, but the ugly corporal ran in screaming again.

"Follow the blue line. Follow the blue line to Vision. Hey you, the black guy in dirty underwear, I said *blue*."

In a room where eye charts papered the wall stood Maynard Wilson. Maynard drove moonshine for a living because he was only seventeen and when arrested, his father and uncles were sure he would be tried as a juvenile and get off with a slap on the wrist. Everything worked out better than even Maynard anticipated when he was eventually caught, because his particular judge actually believed rehabilitation was more than a word. Or so Maynard told me in rapid-fire sentence fragments while the line we were in slowly shortened.

"This sorry son-of-a-bitchin' judge thinks he's smarter than me. Gives me a choice of goin' to work camp till I'm eighteen and then doin' a stretch in Lexington for three more years. *Or*, enlistin' in the service for four years 'cause the military would rehabilitate me."

"Seems to me the military might be a death sentence for you, Maynard."

"If I was normal, maybe. But I ain't normal. See, that's where I outfoxed the old bastard. I tell his bailiff to walk me right on down to the recruiting station and sign me up, all the while knowin' I'm blind in my left eye..."

"So you're thinking once he sees you sign your name and clears your record, you come down here and flunk the physical..."

"...and be free as a bird by sundown with my obligation fulfilled."

"Pretty smart."

"Damn straight. It's genius. We got special sense in Hazard, Kentucky 'cause we're all related."

The line moved quicker and the closer we came to the eye chart, the more Maynard smiled. One by one, recruits peeled off the front end in four directions. They stood frozen, one hand over one eye, then the other. Like a tent revival, the room echoed with insensible tongues. ADWZUXYBLKKGIQVVE. Maynard stepped right. I stepped left. The men in white coats pointed to various rows of letters, which I read perfectly. Leaving the room, I heard the boy from Hazard whimper in the background and the optometrist answer.

"But…I'm blind in my left eye."

"I said, please cover your left eye and read the chart."

By the time my new friend caught me at a traffic light, the only thing going on in my head was a Bob Dylan song from his album *Highway 61 Revisited.* The words danced around flash card images, everything from a cheerleader named Katie to John Wayne driving a bulldozer in some B movie. "God said to Abraham kill me a son. Abe say where ya want this killing done. God say out on Highway 61." Bells and whistles bounced around in my head as the traffic light changed colors.

"Mother Fucker…Mother Fucker. I'm fucked, totally fucked." Maynard seemed disoriented, incapable of getting unfucked. "I'm really fucked. Can you believe how fucked I am? Those fuckers took a blind man…*a blind man for god's sake.*"

"You're not blind. You see twenty-twenty out of your right eye."

"So what?"

"So, you're right handed. It only takes your right eye to sight down a rifle barrel and shoot somebody."

"Jesus, why didn't I think of that."

"Well, I'm used to dealing with unsound logic. Remember I told you, I went to college in Kentucky for a few months."

Both of us laughed and walked down Fourth Street toward the seedy hotel where the government housed inductees and enlistees overnight before shipping them to various boot camps. Along the way, we passed several topless bars and blue movie houses. I had never seen so much untouchable flesh for sale in such a small area of buildings and city blocks.

"Let's get drunk and watch some strippers tonight. Bus don't leave for Parris Island till tomorrow morning late," said Maynard.

"We're too young to drink, dumbass."

"Ain't that a bitch. Old enough to die, but not to get pukin' drunk. Lucky for us I got a quart of daddy's best homemade stuff in my suitcase."

We walked through the lobby of the hotel, past three winos snoozing in dusty chairs, past a hooker who smiled, flicked her tongue snake-like, and winked at us. The desk clerk, a dirty, pock-faced man in a greasy tee shirt, threw a key at Maynard and nodded. A boy about twelve years old kicked and rattled the cigarette machine trying to loosen a pack of smokes. Heat and humidity were everywhere, like a disease. I couldn't see them, but felt them killing every living thing in Louisville, sucking breath and soul away. Only the boy at the cigarette machine had enough strength left to fight back. Each angry punch and kick into the machine was a blow against the uncontrollable spread of infectious summer. But even the boy lost the battle when the glass pane across the front shattered loudly and brought the desk clerk screaming and waving a black jack. The glass crunched under running feet as both the boy and the man ran out a fire door at the back of the hotel.

The dimly lit and narrow hallway that led to room 107 stank of piss and stale beer. I felt vomit rising in my throat. Gagging when the door to the room opened, I rushed past the two beds into the bathroom. Bending double over the toilet, I waited. Nothing happened. Maynard called me to come get a drink. I controlled my urge, and sweating heavily, walked back to the main room.

"Hey, you alright?"

"Got sick to my stomach. It's too damn hot. It's always too hot here in the summer."

"Not near as hot as where we're goin'." Maynard poured two shots of clear liquid into paper cups on the nightstand. "This'll make you feel better fast."

Everyone always remembers the first time they make love. My faith was reaffirmed in this proverb as I tasted Maynard's moonshine. It was my first time making love to good whiskey and I still measure each shot from all the bottles I have drunk across this country and around the world with the taste and effect of that first shot. It seemed to me that corn liquor properly enjoyed, like sex, caused transcendence from one plane of being to another. The first shot frightened me till it hit the back of my tongue, and then the hint of honey and vanilla rode a one hundred and forty proof flame into the pit of my stomach where is nested and spread its warmth along every fiber of my being. By the third shot, I was a hummingbird draining the nectar of life from a rose bush. Two hours later when Maynard finally mumbled, "Let's go see some naked women," I was a walking orgasm.

Sauntering out into the sweltering Louisville night, passing pawnshops, coffee shops, topless bars, and one combination lawyer-bail bond office, we finally stopped in front of a worn, red brick movie theater. The neon marquee spelled out *Art Films and Live Girls*, and directly below those words, the title of the current film, *Debbie Does Dallas – in color.* I watched my heavy set and slightly bearded companion thrust both hands into the pockets of *OshKosh Bigosh* denim overalls as if the blue-eyed young man might need to squeeze a sigh from somewhere below his stomach.

"This must be our place," Maynard said.

"It doesn't look like much on the outside."

"These places never do. They spend all their money hirin' quality entertainment."

A bored girl with yellow skin and too much blue eyeliner took our money and promised with a wink that we would enjoy the show. Inside, the air was cool and stank like stale popcorn and Wild Irish Rose wine. Six men and one person who could have been either gender were spread out in various sections, which seemed to give them each a feeling of privacy. A man with hair the color and viscosity of used motor oil came from behind a dirty white curtain and stood above them on a wooden stage.

Ladies and Gentlemen – His tired voice resonated through the auditorium – *You are about to see a live show that will dazzle, deprave, and drain your very soul. Miss Chastity Flame will perform her famous fire dance without so much as a shoestring covering her voluptuous body. She walks, she talks, she crawls on her belly like a reptile. She'll shake it up one side and roll it down the other. She can keep you home at night without baking a cake. Please welcome Miss Chastity Flame.*

"This here's what we came to Louisville for big boy," Maynard whispered.

A middle aged woman strutted across the stage as the Coasters hit song *Little Egypt* played loudly in the background. Her tits were huge and heavy, hanging almost to her waist. They were the biggest tits I had ever seen. The single spotlight outlined blue veins on her legs and a Y of black pubic hair. She moved in slow jerks, like a machine whose batteries were in dire need of recharging.

As the song reached its bridge chord, Chastity moaned and fell on her knees, exposing the lips of her vagina. Reaching right, she picked up a coat hanger that had been straightened and a Zippo left by the emcee off the floor and lit the cotton ball stuck on one end of the hanger. The moaning grew louder. She ground her wide ass into the floor and brought the fire down to floor level. Chastity hunched the flame. The seven people squirmed. Some rubbed their crotches. I was hypnotized, motionless. Maynard screamed, "Fuck the fire baby. Fuck the fire."

And she did, as if his voice was the voice of God and she was Joan of Arc. Chastity rammed the wire rod deep inside, moaned, and extracted a smoking piece of wet cotton.

On the walk back to the hotel, I kept seeing Chastity as a young woman who needed to be rescued. She was studying ballet, caring for her sick mother, earning money to pay for her crippled brother's operation by stripping. I felt sad that circumstance beyond control forced such a nice person to work in a filthy place. I hated life as the whiskey wore off and wished that I could do something for this poor, mistreated woman. It never occurred to me that she might have had a choice, any more than the little boy who murdered the cigarette machine had one. This weakness in my character, the willingness to see all women as victims in need of rescue and to try and rescue the most needy, would prove a costly emotional flaw as I grew into my twenties.

By 7a.m. the next morning, my headache had erased all thought of Chastity. The sadness and anger over her fate was replaced by a violent urge to wretch. I did. I did again and again, hugging the toilet bowl as if it was a steering wheel.

"Drivin' the old moonshine bus, I see. Well, hurry up and finish puking. We gotta eat some breakfast before we travel."

I puked again.

On the long ride to Parris Island, South Carolina, Maynard and I became close. The emotional intensity of each individual experience became a shared intensity and time sped up. In seventeen hours we had known each other for seventeen years. This particular phenomenon got repeated often during the war and now, after the war, I couldn't even remember the names of Marines I swore were closer to me than brothers. Once the Greyhound bus passed the guard shack and the security fence at the Marine Corps Recruit Depot on Parris Island and stopped at the side of a white-washed building, I lost Maynard in the chaos the way I might have lost a ball cap in a violent windstorm.

A man wearing a large brimmed "Smoky the Bear" hat and with drool speckled around his lips charged onto the parade deck. He screamed, cursed, kicked, and pushed the entire busload of pimpled recruits into four ragtag lines.

"My name to you is Drill Instructor, Sir, but my friends call me Spasdick. You WILL know why before this two months is over. I hate all of you scudsy, pimple-faced, maggot mother fuckers." Spasdick screamed as he trotted up and down between the rows of frightened young men, including me. "Your mothers are all whores and your fathers are all queers. In the next eight weeks I will make men of you, or I WILL kill you. Do you understand me?"

"YES SIR, DRILL INSTRUCTOR SIR." The entire group shouted in perfect harmony. Three recruits pissed in their pants, Someone giggled from the tension. Spasdick slapped him so hard he almost fell. I forced myself not to feel sorry for him. The possibility of Death began coming into me like an injection of emotional Novocain, numbing my senses so that whatever happened in the future could be absorbed without pain.

Once boot camp was over, Maynard and I were sent to the same outfit in Vietnam, the 3rd Battalion of the 9th Marine Regiment. I went straight to an infantry platoon, but Maynard, with his special talent, was assigned to the motor pool in Da Nang. In a way, I was glad for my young friend who had not yet celebrated his eighteenth birthday because driving supply trucks along Highway 1 was a hell of a lot safer than beating the bush for Viet Cong and Maynard didn't deserve to be in combat. He had been a victim of a circumstance who, unlike me, had to choose between a rock and a hard place. It didn't seem fair, even though Maynard had put himself in that circumstance.

When I came back to the rear area in Da Nang after my first long search and destroy operation, I went to the motor pool to find my buddy and share a few beers. The First Sergeant in charge told me in a casual tone that Maynard was running a load of c-rations up to a fire base called "The Rockpile" when his truck had run over a mine and the clutch plate got buried in Maynard's forehead.

So much for Kentucky boys with an angle, I thought as I heard the clanging of blacksmith tools. So much for believing that life existed for your benefit, no matter where you came from. Whatever force was out there turning the world, making the sun shine and the wind blow – the one my father always called *luck* – didn't pay much attention to the people affected by the normal operation of the planet or the intersection of those people with their angles.

Monty was untying his leather apron and backing away from the horse.

"You been awful quiet the last twenty minutes. Didn't mean to spook you with all that Vietnam talk."

"You didn't. I just daydream a lot anymore. Hell, don't you think about pussy?"

"Not since I got married. Walk that horse down the shed row. I want to make sure everything's even and he ain't sore from the trimming."

I walked Kentucky Honey back and forth twice. The little colt felt good and bucked and pranced to show it. When Monty was satisfied that the shoes were right, we put the horse away. I packed his feet with a mud mixture of clay, Epsom salts, and Absorbine to draw out any tenderness or excess heat and covered the mud with a square patch of heavy paper cut from an old feed sack to hold it in place. Then, I hung the hayrack on the stall doorjamb, and walked over to the grandstand area to watch a few races as a distraction. It didn't work very well, so I drank and drank some more at the Bridgeview Tavern. The tavern stood on Highway 41 South just over the bridge that separated Evansville, Indiana, and Henderson, Kentucky. I had taken a room at a nearby motel for the duration of the meet. At midnight I had reached such a state of intoxication that my mind held no more memories of Vietnam. However, no one knew that a thing called post-traumatic stress existed back then. By the time I left the tavern and returned to the motel, images began to seep across that border between unconscious and conscious like dark, dirty oil.

Chapter Eight

PTSD

Monica's Motel attempted to appear as a Swiss chalet hidden away in the snowcapped Alps full of beautiful skiers. As many imitations did, it looked absurd and completely out of place in the weed and mosquito infested bottom land of the Ohio River. The dreary brown façade was covered with moss and chipped beige paint around the window sills. The parking lot lights cast a jaundiced pall over rusted out pickups and battered cars. The neon sign flashed above the entrance at different times and in different order like an alphabet code – *M—I—A—N—O—C—S—'*– and at the front desk, Monica herself slumped over a newspaper, maybe asleep or maybe reading.

The hum of the electric transformers that ringed the building and the clang and clatter of cheap air conditioners filled the night air with mechanical harshness. As I entered my room rented by the week, the familiar stench of dirty socks, stale cigarette smoke, and the decay of a hundred souls that passed through it before rose to meet me. Swamped by lonely odors my knees buckled, and I stumbled over the mislaid carpet, cursing.

The lack of a concrete understanding as to why one person dies and not another at the random whim of some unseen energy terrified me every day and kept me awake most nights till my mind was numb enough with exhaustion or alcohol or both that it put itself to sleep. This confusion was stoked by the fire of survivor's guilt. I carried it every day, along with the knowledge that our country invaded another country, killed millions of civilians, displaced millions more, and reduced an ancient civilization to rubble. The only thing we liberated was morality, set free from its place in the conscience by the death of innocents. Survivor's Guilt – a psychobabble term meaning I had not paid for my sins. I lived and breathed every minute of every day on time borrowed from corpses, American and Vietnamese.

I lost friends who were closer than brothers and would have traded places with any of them gladly. Still, this self-loathing did nothing to answer the most important question of any survivor of any war. Why me? No one, not one single person I had spoken with or one single book I had read gave me the slightest understanding of the sacrificial choices made by the god of war. Taking a bottle of Jim Beam from the dresser, I laid on the bed and turned the TV to an infomercial for Ronco Vegamatic blenders.

How fitting that life should be reduced to working a menial job on a racetrack seven days a week and listening to the machinations of a barker in the black night. I stared at the luminescent dial on the motel clock radio. It was already 3:30 AM. The fluorescent light in the bathroom hummed with the sound of a waterfall. Ordinarily, the soft noise would have hypnotized me, lulling me into a somnambulant trance that laughingly passed for sleep. The present rummaged through the past again, almost as if it was searching for something the past had put away in a drawer underneath a bunch of old clothes. It felt like a seizure. Even the bourbon had no effect. One minute I giggled like a child at the sweet scent of thoroughbred horses and strong liniment on my clothes. The next minute, I paced the floor to keep my heart from exploding. My pulse raced and I moved to keep up with it.

Reaching for cigarettes and finding an empty pack, I crumpled it into a ball and threw it at the TV as the Ronco Vegamatic man twisted his face into a wall-eyed grimace and appeared ready to cry. As if by the grace of some good god, this miraculous machine – cruncher, smasher, blender, and creator of joyful juice – could be made available at this late, or early depending on your habits, hour along with thirty-seven appendages and a recipe book for the mere low price of an ordinary can of V-8.

I had another pack of Camels on the night stand by the bed.

Groping in the dim blue glow, I felt the safety of the cellophane, opened the fresh pack, lit one, and saw the white cap from the Beam bottle in the refracted light of the dying match. I unscrewed the cap and took another drink of Jim Beam, repeating this ritual in a thoughtless fog until at last the world outside got brighter. I checked the clock in the motel room again. 5:34AM. Night wore against the rough edges of my mind like sandpaper. Dawn began to seep in the window gray and vague almost without my notice. I had never closed my eyes really except to blink. This was the longest sleepless patch I'd been through in several months. At first when the War ended, I believed I might be insane. I lived daily with the greatest anxiety I had ever known – fear of being locked in a dirty VA hospital drooling and heavily medicated without the ability to even remember who I was. Then, I read an article in some self-help magazine that said if you had enough presence of mind to think you were insane you probably weren't.

Little by little over the past five years, I accepted the memories as part of present life and learned to deal with them on the inside while performing this normal routine of living on the outside. It was a matter of learning to live in two places at once, not necessarily easy, but doable if I kept the illusion of tight control in my mind. Occasionally things got out of hand because a room was too quiet, I was too tired, or drank too much, or not enough. Yesterday afternoon had been bad. The blacksmith, Monty, had forced the past to rise in me like vomit with his incessant questions and silly reasoning.

Now, it was morning again and time to go back to the track and do my job. I hadn't reached the point of having a hangover yet. The bourbon had worn off enough that I wasn't drunk and not enough to make my head ache. I thought a hot shower might renew me. The water steamed and hissed. The nozzle was old and let out a small, shrill shriek that sounded like an animal caught in a trap. I held my head under the hot stream, letting the noise wash over me. This was one of those days when I felt like just another broken toy soldier.

Toweling off, I dressed. It was ten minutes till six and Dan expected me at the barn by six. The heat, already visible, fell from the sky to the asphalt in a curtain. It was like looking at the world through wax paper. By the time I got to my pickup truck, the clean shirt was soaked with sweat. I was hungry and sick, but mostly tired. I was very tired and the day had just begun.

***

Everything seemed normal as I pulled up in my truck. Dan knelt beneath the racing stable's horses one at a time and ran his hands up and down their front legs, making sure none had rapped a tendon or injured themselves in some other way during the night. All the horses had their heads buried in the feed tubs rooting around in their breakfast oats. Barrel, the huge frog-eyed drunk, lumbered along the waist high outside wall of the barn where the water buckets hung across from each stall after being removed. Stopping at the individual buckets, the big man dumped out the old water, scrubbed the insides with a stiff brush and refilled them with water from the hose and a scoop of electrolytes. When the horses finished morning exercise on the track, they would have fresh water to sip during the cooling out process as they walked around the barn. Hector and Octavio dragged muck baskets and pitchforks into stalls and began forking dirty straw. Wally rolled a cigarette.

"You're ten minutes late, boy," called Dan. as he crawled from a stall and stood stiffly.

"Sorry boss, didn't sleep good and when I did go to sleep, it was hard waking up."

"Excuses are like assholes. Everybody's got one and they all smell. And, you smell like a fucking brewery. Get the gear and tack on Kentucky Honey. I want him schooled in the starting gate early before the track gets crowded. Don't screw this up."

"That won't happen, boss."

"Not if you do your job right."

In the tack room, I pulled a snaffle D-bit and a bridle off a nail and slung it over my shoulder. As I picked up an exercise saddle and a clean saddle towel, Wally came in and grabbed two rolls of vet wrap.

"Boss gonna bandage his back legs?" I asked.

"Yeah, he don't want no cuts on the back pasterns in case Angel pulls the horse up too fast. Excuses are like assholes, assholes I say."

"Shut up, you little prick. I'm getting a headache that won't quit. That squeal you call a voice is about to make my fucking head explode."

"Barrel got head for breakfast."

"What?"

"Head for breakfast, from the preacher woman."

"Bullshit."

"Bullshit, I say he did. She said she couldn't fuck me though 'cause she had acute angina. I said I'm glad something's cute 'cause your tits are sure ugly. What's angina?"

"It's heart pain. It means you could have a heart attack."

"Shit, is that all. I've had pains in my chest for years, so has Barrel. Ain't had no attacks."

"Your time will come. Everybody's does."

I found the piece of flannel I was looking for. Dan screamed, "Wally, bring me those bandages, NOW." The little man ran down the shed row and I wondered, watching him go, if Wally really did have heart trouble. Everyone made choices that influenced life and the way you lived affected your death.

"Make sure you get his tongue tied real good. I'm going to get my stopwatch and head for the rail. Jesus, you stink."

"I'm okay."

"You'd better be."

Chapter Nine

Kentucky Honey Falls in Love

Small fans, wired up in the individual stalls to keep the horses cool, hummed. Some of the geldings and fillies hung their heads over nylon stall webbings and pulled mouthfuls of light green timothy hay from nylon racks with crackling and crunching sounds. After tacking Kentucky Honey, I took a minute and checked on my father's horses. The three we brought over from River Downs were all named after family members and were still unraced two-year-olds.

Of the three, a big, sickle-hocked gelding called Sanden King approached racing fitness quicker than either the filly named Huffy Lady or the stud colt, Jim's Jungle Joy. The colt seemed skittish and frail to me. Under normal circumstances, the course of wisdom would have been to castrate him and let him run as a gelding. Without the excess testosterone, there was a good chance he would put on weight and begin to focus on the business of running. But, my father had simple dreams that drove many of his decisions. He wanted happiness for me and a champion stud to fulfill his breeding hopes. Consequently, while the thought of making me a gelding must have crossed his mind on a daily basis, he fought the idea fervently regarding Jim's Jungle Joy.

I liked the filly best. She enjoyed running better than the other two. Many people often confuse ability and desire, especially in race horses. Jim's Jungle Joy had proven many times that he ran faster than Huffy Lady by himself. All it took for that was a stopwatch. But, even though races are timed, they aren't about time. While at River Downs, Barry worked these two side by side on three occasions. Each time, the filly refused to allow the colt ahead of her. Always, he spit the bit and quit trying. He had the athleticism and she had the grace and class. I knew instantly which would become the better race horse. My one fear resided in her conformation – her skeletal structure. Huffy Lady's front legs turned in. She was pigeon-toed and any slight deviation from perfectly straight angles could make her injury prone with the weight and stress of racing. But, on this particular morning, my first on the new job, all of them looked healthy and happy.

Dan paraded Kentucky Honey around the barn. The colt pranced nervously showing off his new shoes that Monty had fitted perfectly the day before. I admired Dan. He never missed a day the entire time we worked together, an amazing feat considering that he drank a bottle of vodka every afternoon after five or six beers with his lunch. As a victim of alcohol poisoning, which means victim of my own stupidity, I regarded his ability with admiration, if not awe. Once after drinking a gallon of Boar's Head Apple flavored wine in the Marine Corps, I awoke under my bunk covered in puke, dry heaving with a fever of one hundred and three degrees. Of course, that may have had more to do with the strange ingredients that must have been in a bottle of wine costing $1.59 plus tax than with my capacity for holding liquor.

We waited on the exercise rider to show up and take Kentucky Honey to the track. The colt belonged to a fellow from northern Kentucky who owned a string of restaurants that were called "smorgasbords" in the vernacular of the early 1970's. We call them all-you-can-eat buffets now. Honey was unraced and had been scheduled to practice loading and breaking out of the starting gate. State racing commission rules made it mandatory for any unraced horse to come out of the gate correctly three times before running a race. The "schooling" cut down on injuries in the afternoons when ten or twelve one thousand pound animals had to be loaded and sprung at the start of each race. This was Honey's first trip to the gate.

Occasionally, when passing one of the stalls that housed other stud horses, including Jim's Jungle Joy, Dan had to duck. They all ran at the webbing, thrust their chests against it, and extended long necks into the walking ring, nipping playfully at anyone who passed to prove their dominance. It paid to stay alert because a playful bite from a thoroughbred stud could remove a piece of flesh the size of an orange. On the other hand, I enjoyed watching them because it meant that they were "feeling their oats" or the power and pleasure of being well-conditioned, full of testosterone, and focused on running fast.

The Hispanic boys, Hector and Octavio, found Barrel. The two boys worked down the line of stalls on the west side of the barn. The fat man rolled the wheelbarrow loaded with dirty straw to the muck pit, dumped it, and returned to the barn for refills. Wally held a grooming tray filled with brushes, currycombs, rags, hoof picks, and various liniments and leg rubs pretending to be busy. I grabbed a pitchfork so I could lay down clean straw as the horses took their turns on the track. Jade appeared at the corner of the barn on her Appaloosa pony ready to escort the little chestnut colt and his rider to their appointment at the starting gate.

I smiled, not only because the sight of Jade's fat ass astride her pony created several comic images as to how she might have mounted, but also because this was the one time of the day when all was right in the world. Everyone and everything started with a sense of purpose, fresh and willing, as yet unfucked by the randomness of uncontrollable circumstance waiting to drop in the spinning roulette wheel of a new day.

Angel Lopez arrived at 6:15. According to Dan, Angel was a longtime friend. He rode races, but not very well. The only thing that got him a lot of mounts was his naturally light weight. Angel had never weighed over a hundred and ten pounds in his life. Dan respected his courage. The son-of-a-bitch would get on anything with four legs, no matter how crippled, or how rank, and ride the best race he could with limited abilities. He wasn't afraid to take the inside rail turning for home, or stick and drive up behind a wall of horses on a crippled horse. These things came to me by way of conversation. In person and up close, Angel's face was round and deeply tanned. A long scar ran across his left cheek from below the eye to the bottom of his sideburn. When he caught me admiring it, Angel smiled and with his black eyes twinkling said, "a woman in my youth, mi amiga con los ojos tristes. You must have some scars also, I think."

***

To discern the difference between too much summer heat and the first rush of desire requires a subtlety of reasoning unattainable in most young males of any warm-blooded species. Either one makes you sweat. Both blur your vision and cause you to tremble. You want to resist the pull of instinct but the body is too weak to respond. So with every fiber of control gone, you step into the abyss. *If* someone stands over your prostrate form hosing you down, it was the sun's heat. If you are alone in a crowd of strangers, skinned and shattered by regret, then it was desire.

Certainly, heat played a role in Kentucky Honey's first trip to the starting gate and also the wind, which was strong enough to mingle straw, liniment, bad coffee, sweat, leather, and manure with the air and create a humid soup full of anticipation and possibilities. There was lways the wind dragging the sun behind it at Ellis Park. For some unknown reason, the early spring thunderstorms had outlived their life expectancy and conjured up rudely the pre-dawn breezes of these Midwestern dog days. I watched closely and the air seemed to lift Angel Lopez out of the saddle as he loped the two-year-old colt over the sand and clay once around for a warm-up and back where Jade rested on her pony along the outside rail at the top of the mile chute. The gentle pressure molded his face into a smile that the strain on his arms and legs did not appear to diminish. The colt and he were cogs in the same cosmic machine even though on separate planes of being.

I couldn't have asked for a better seat for the workout unless I had been in the saddle. My view of the starting gate was clear and unrestrained by horses or buildings. At Ellis Park, the track circles from the finish line in front of the grandstand back to the finish line over a distance of one and one-eighth miles. Since races are run at varying lengths and since turns are where most injuries occur, whoever engineered this particular track, built a straight chute that ran in line with the main track for a furlong, or an eighth of a mile, on the first, or clubhouse, turn. Consequently, all races run at a distance of one mile or less could start from the gate in a straight line reducing the risk of two turns while allowing maximum speed. The flood levee that protected the track from the Ohio River ran parallel to this chute. Between the levee and the chute, a row of barns in a neighborhood that Hard Boots affectionately called "the bottoms" housed Dan Wilson's public stable every year along with several other Ellis Park regulars.

As Jade waited on the track by the seven-furlong pole for Angel to circle once, Dan and I leaned on the outside rail about thirty feet from the starting gate, which sat on its wheels out of the way of the main training area at the far end of the chute. Angel and Honey pulled together in different directions. The colt leaned heavily into the snaffle bit. The man stood straight in the irons, tugging upward evenly on both reins. One pulled through instinct, the other with respect, and both delighted in the sense of competition. Without the set of rings and the leather yoke around his massive chest to keep his head bowed and give the rider leverage, Kentucky Honey would have run off and kept running until his four legs turned to jelly. It would have been a good trip for a couple of miles though, horse and man flowing free, barely touching the surface of the track. Humans had to come to a belief that nothing was more sacred than the buzz of adrenaline in your blood and a warm wind in your face. The horse knew that instinctively. It was part of what made thoroughbreds great runners.

As they rounded the clubhouse, Angel slowed the horse down and guided him through the heavy morning traffic toward the chute as other horses galloped by. The colt tossed his head side to side vigorously in an effort to break the rider's strong grip on the reins. It was more of a game than anything else. The jockey eased him down to a jog along the outside rail and began to post up and down like a piston, barely touching his seat on the exercise saddle as Kentucky Honey pegged first one leg then another into the soft clay and sand surface.

They turned off the main track and walked through the gap into the area containing the starting gate, the young horse broke into a foamy white sweat along his neck and under the saddle towel, a sure sign that he was either overheating or getting very nervous, or both.

"Ole Honey's starting to wash out pretty fucking good." Wally spat as he spoke.

"Shut up before you jinx his shit," growled Barrel and filled his cheek with a wad of Red Man from a wrinkled foil pouch.

"Both of you shut the fuck up. You're neither one worth two dead flies."

That phrase – ain't worth two dead flies – happened to be a common expression of Dan's whenever he felt stressed by something. Forty years later I continue to repeat the admonition as if it were scripture. He waved Jade over. She jogged her pony quickly toward him.

"Go hook Angel up and help him get that randy little colt to the gate. What the fuck do I pay you for, goddammit."

"Yeah, goddammit."

Dan shot Wally a withering look and the parrot-like mimicry ceased immediately.

"Don't you worry, Baby. I'll handle it."

Jade loped her pony away. With an elegance and grace hard to believe possible from someone her size, she ran the pony alongside Kentucky Honey's left rein, stood in the stirrups, leaned forward out over her own mount's neck, and hooked a short leather lead strap through the D on the bit where it entered the colt's mouth. This accomplished two things effectively. The company calmed the excitable race horse and the strap allowed Jade to control the bridle so Angel could relax his grip for a few minutes. The pony and the thoroughbred took off side by side, but within a few strides, the thoroughbred was kicking and bucking and nipping at Jade's right leg. She shook the lead shank, rattling the bit in Kentucky Honey's mouth and slowed her pony back to a trot.

The huge starting gate with its twelve steel cages and its banging green doors that sprung open like monster jaws, with its crew of strange men scurrying around in all directions like soldier ants and its clanging bells, awaited them fifty yards in the distance. They were passing us when I noticed the colt begin to roll his eyes as if he might have a seizure, fountains of white foamed sweat churned, like whipped cream from an aerosol can, out of his chestnut-colored coat. I paid absolutely no attention to the John Deere tractor used to pull the gate from one location to another. It was parked where it was every morning along the inside rail near the starter's tower. Neither did Dan. More importantly, neither did Angel or Jade. But, Kentucky Honey fell in love at first sight.

As they came around to the back of the gate where the colt would be loaded, a member of the gate crew stepped forward and Jade passed her pony strap to him. He led Kentucky Honey a few steps away and circled him back toward one of the open cages in the starting gate. His intention was to walk the horse into the cage with the rider mounted, hesitate a moment, and then walk him out the front as a way to familiarize the young colt with something new and strange. There were to be no bells. The front had already been opened as well so as not to startle the animal. Horses are skittish by nature and this was merely a walk through. It would allow Honey the opportunity to smell and feel and see his new environment in a relaxed way.

The only one misunderstanding all this seemed to be the colt, and he certainly was not relaxed. As they passed the John Deere tractor, his penis shot out of its sheath like a fired rocket. Erect, hard as steel, as huge as a baseball bat, it began slapping against the underside of Honey's belly. The colt reared straight into the air on his hind legs, ripping the short pony strap from the man on the ground's grip and throwing Angel off backward into the tractor's engine. Still in a state of passion, Kentucky Honey came down on all fours rider-less, whirled to his left and in one jump mounted the tractor. With his front legs resting on the rear tires, his heaving chest pressed against the tractor seat, Kentucky Honey got busy with what appeared to be the rear axle.

Everything took place within a few seconds, all in one big motion and quick enough that no one had the chance to respond. Several other members of the gate crew rushed to peel the horse off his cold, hard lover, as did Jade on her pony. Angel pulled himself up off the track, but we discovered shortly that the collision with the tractor motor had broken his right arm. Dan and the rest of us rushed toward the scene. Kentucky Honey, off the metal beast and encircled by wild men with flapping arms and squealing like a gaggle of geese, only became more frightened, rearing and striking at the air like a shadow boxer until Dan leaped in quickly and hooked a lead shank across his nose and led him back to his stall. That very afternoon, after the colt's scratches and lacerations were treated, the veterinarian made a special trip to the barn and readjusted his attitude forever with a scalpel and a pair of scissors, quickly snipping the two offensive little globes from their chords as a gardener might prune rotted fruit from a tree. Hector carried them away in a stainless steel bucket and fed them to a circle of feral cats out by the levee.

Once his focus had been directed to the task of running, our former little stud horse went on to become a fairly productive gelding that earned his owner some fun and profit, provided the crowds with some excitement, and lived a relatively content life, at least while on the race track. Like many events I only witnessed, this one remained locked away in my memory, disconnected from the stream of actual experiences that make up the river of my life. Thirty plus years later, I realized the message Kentucky Honey had attempted to share with me at some primal level unrecognizable to me at the time. True love is a privilege afforded only the spontaneous and the fearless. It is one of the few energy sources powerful enough to shock the soul back to life. A child who sticks his finger into a light socket will receive enough voltage to awaken all his senses and his world will become larger afterward. Falling helplessly, impulsively, and naturally in love without regard for velocity generates a similar sensation and, like an electric shock, love leads often to regret.

Chapter Ten

It's All About the Finish Line

Regardless of how much you love horses, your success as a trainer in charge of a public stable ends up being about whether you win enough races to support the business and attract new clients. The Ellis Park race meet had been successful for the Dan Wilson Racing Stable and surrendered its days gracefully to Latonia for the month of September. We shipped to the small track in Florence, Kentucky, just across the river from Cincinnati, Ohio, and spent the next four weeks looking for easy races. We found a few and earned more money. Sanden King, one of my father's horses, won his first race there. It's called breaking your maiden because the race is run between horses that have yet to win. You would have thought it was the Kentucky Derby. My father, a caravan of friends, and several relatives drove the four hours from southwest Indiana, drank beer, smoked cigars, cashed bets, and got their pictures taken in the winner's circle with the big black gelding. The winner's share of the purse wasn't much. But, it didn't matter, not in the least. Nothing matters when a dream deferred becomes a dream realized except that moment in time.

I felt the excitement myself in the hum of the crisp autumn night air. I liked it very much, not the simple victory alone but the fact that my father seemed to approve of my current lifestyle. No matter how violent the verbal conflict between us, I needed his approval all of *his* life. My freedom, the completeness of self all of us strive for, seemed impossible until he passed away. This may be the seed of Freud's famous oedipal complex, at least as metaphor. After returning from Vietnam and joining a movement called Vietnam Veterans Against the War, we got into a brutal screaming match about my lack of patriotism and ungratefulness. When the heat subsided, I rushed to my apartment and loaded a box full of trophies, ribbons, commendations, plaques, and medals, all earned by me in the first two decades of my life.

"These are yours, not mine," I screamed, as he sat behind his huge desk in the car dealership. "I earned them for you and I don't want them anymore." It was a moment of realization and confusion for us both. I set the box on an empty chair and left for somewhere a few hours later. I don't remember where that was anymore, maybe Mexico or maybe New York again, just somewhere away from my current life.

***

Even though I enjoyed the rush of winning, my father and I were getting along, and Dan seemed happy with the way I ran the barn, a familiar restlessness returned to the edges of my conscious mind. It probed, a synaptic intruder, seeking a weak spot to enter and plunder whatever joy might be hiding there. However, a slight difference made this current wave of existential dread more bearable. I didn't feel absolutely lost as I had on other occasions since the war. I had no particular wanderlust driving me toward New York or Mexico as in the past. My agitation bonded with a purpose this time. Indeed, I wanted and needed to be doing something *else*, but this time I knew what that was. I should run my own public racing stable, train my own horses, be in control of my own destiny. Mostly, I craved the rush that came when a horse won a race, the self-congratulatory impulse that came from getting it to the winner's circle with the help of your own expertise.

Theoretically, my on-the-job training had only begun. I was a novice in race track terms. Most men spent years learning how to mix a healthy diet, handle typical leg problems – bone chips, bruised feet, shin splints, bowed tendons, torn ligaments, strains – that went with racing, and then condition each animal according to its individual physical requirements in order to reach its highest competing level. Unforeseen details clouded every decision with doubt and understanding anatomy and nutrition and horse care only made you a good groom. Trainers had to know what races to enter, what medications were legal, basic economics and bookkeeping, how to supervise employees, how to schmooze wealthy clients, and how to recognize talented horses with potential before they ever ran a race.

Even with all these skills mastered, very few horsemen achieved the most from their businesses.

Like writing, painting, sculpting, or any other form of art-making, to be really good at what he does a horse trainer must transcend craft. He needs to make subjective decisions frequently that cannot be measured or quantified in any particular way. This requires instinct rather than skill. Skill sharpens instinct but it can't stand alone. For example, skill won't teach you to recognize heart in a young horse. You may recognize coordination, speed, and stamina, but it takes a special kind of intuition to look at a horse and feel the grace and desire inside it that will keep that horse running when others have spit the bit and quit. Dan knew two of my father's horses, Sanden King and Huffy Lady, had that type of class and Jim's Jungle Joy didn't, even though he was much faster than both in training situations. This was the same feeling I had at River Downs when working for Barry. The fact that Dan seemed blessed with an intuition that escaped Barry, my first employer, and the possibility that I had the same instinct excited me. Even though Barry had been much more deliberate and had taken first-class care of all his horses, I don't remember him ever winning a race in his entire short-lived career. The question was – did I have enough magic to win races? Did I have the stuff to become something more than a good caretaker, to translate my instinct into action?

I read a magazine article somewhere about Lucien Lauren after Secretariat won the Belmont Stakes by almost a quarter of a mile in 1973 and clinched the Triple Crown, maybe one of the most spectacular performances in the history of horse racing. After winning a close race in the Preakness over Sham, his main rival, Big Red deserved a rest and most good trainers would have given him one, training him only lightly for three weeks up to the Belmont. Traditional wisdom dictated that these three races over a five week period were too grueling for even great horses to win consistently, especially if those horses had been over-raced or over-trained. The lack of Triple Crown winners over a century vindicated that idea. Lauren was certainly aware of this. Yet, he ignored tradition with Secretariat. He worked the great runner like a plow horse. Something akin to the flash of inspiration Beethoven must have felt when he wrote the 9th symphony directed this eccentric little man to defy all common sense, even his own. Knowing that if his horse ran poorly he would go down in history as a fool, Lauren followed the magic in his brain into an unknown realm. Why? Because he was more than a craftsman, he was an artist and he felt what Big Red wanted as well as knowing what the horse needed. The result remains one of the great athletic achievements in the 20ᵗʰ century. Secretariat destroyed the field, including Sham, by 34 lengths.

Once Dan explained his belief that Huffy Lady would be a better race horse than the bigger, stronger, faster colt because she had class, I began paying close attention to everything being done to condition horses physically on the track by as many trainers as I could and as often as I could. How was it possible to recognize class? What did the word mean really? I understood the result of having it. That seemed simple enough. I had recognized it before. If the word could be defined similar to its meaning in human terms, it might be described as courage, integrity, passion, and righteousness combined and creating something greater than the sum of those parts. One of the greatest compliments my father gave anyone was to say, "That's a fellow with a lot of class. Everything he does is high class." Of course, my father used to tell me as a teenager, "Son, you sure have a lot of class, but it's all low."

When Jim's Jungle Joy breezed, or ran at race-like speeds along the inside rail, once every four or five mornings instead of his usual two mile gallop, his speeds indicated a lot of ability. He covered three furlongs shading 36 seconds regularly. His last work had been at five furlongs in a blistering minute. He approached racing fitness rapidly and Dan would soon enter him in a maiden race. Huffy Lady exercised on basically the same schedule but her times were much slower. On their last breeze before he started looking for a race, Dan decided to work them head-to-head, giving each a feel for competition. The riders were told to keep them together till the last eighth of a mile and then turn them loose. I watched the training exercise. When Huffy Lady got her head, she simply pinned her ears and ran away from the colt as she had done in the past at River Downs. On the other hand, he seemed devastated, spit the bit, and quit running almost entirely.

"That filly's got a lot of class," Dan said. The future would prove his assessment correct. Huffy Lady went on over the next three years to win many races, often beating horses that were bigger, faster, and stronger. The little colt, on the other hand, never broke his maiden and ended up someone's pet within the very next year. When I asked Dan exactly what class was, he couldn't explain it. When I asked him a sure fire way to recognize it, he said, "You just remember that time means nothing unless you're in prison."

I had read a dozen books written by famous horsemen on the care and conditioning of thoroughbreds, a dozen more by vets on anatomy, nutrition, and leg care. I watched everything Dan did closely, including paper work and judging which races to enter which horses. I lived on the track in a tack room and worked seven days a week ten hours a day. I lived horses. My intensity to detail became obsessive. I experimented with various ways to run bandages on ankles and knees and what medicines worked best where. Dan taught me how to give injections in the veins and muscles of horses and what medicines had to safely go where. This practice was illegal, but a common one for trainers for practical reasons. For example, veterinarians charged twenty dollars to give 20 cents worth of an anti-inflammatory medication, Phenalbutazone or "Bute" as we called it, and it was a standard pre-race medication.

If he trained one horse with long slow gallops, others with short fast works, and still others with Jade and her pony leading them around rider-less, I made sure to question why. Even though I had devoted only six months of my life to this business, I believed my education complete enough to train my father's horses and maybe pick up another client or two. What I lacked was the confidence that comes from experience. Could I recognize class in a race horse consistently? Did I have enough intuition to crank a runner up to peak performance and not wind that horse too tight with too much exercise? Was I inspired artist enough to adapt my methods or create new ones based on the personality and ability of each individual thoroughbred?

The path to those answers required convincing my father I had become more than his war damaged son, that I had become an adult. Also, it meant taking income away from Dan who had been more than generous to me with his knowledge and time. My father proved to be easily persuaded. He loved me and wanted me to be a successful businessman, as he was. I had proven myself completely useless in the automobile business when I first came home from Vietnam, mainly because the mundane minutiae involved in money dealings of any kind drove me into fits of rage. We simply agreed that he would handle the books, insurance, taxes, and speak with perspective clients, and I would deal with the seven-day-a-week job of training horses. On the other hand, I wasn't sure how to approach Dan until something occurred in the spring of the very next year that made my leaving his employ seem less a desertion and more an escape.

Chapter Eleven

The Nature of Desire

Nothing arouses the romantic nature of a disillusioned masculinity more than the sweet scent of alfalfa and Kentucky bluegrass tangled in a whiff of Absorbine and mucked straw. Keeneland Race Track in Lexington, Kentucky, blends that perfume perfectly every April during its short spring meeting. I always loved racing horses there during my gypsy era and that love affair began while working with Dan and his crew. Dan took a chance on me. I was a young man, college dropout, home from war with a giant chip on my shoulder. He and his girlfriend, Jade, taught me a lot of important things about horses, and some very strange things about the nature of desire and how it often overrides all other human qualities, especially common sense.

Let me illustrate one example of many. We had hauled one of the horses he paid me to groom from his barn at Churchill Downs to run on the Keeneland race card one April afternoon in 1976. The trip from Louisville to Lexington along I-75 took less than two hours, mostly ridden in silence except for Jade's occasional off key caterwauling to some outlaw country singer – Waylon Jennings, I believe. Dan chain-smoked Tareyton cigarettes and patted the dash of his new two-tone blue GMC three-quarter ton pickup, as if the vehicle were a new hunting dog or small child. I read billboards and checked to make sure the filly we were racing this day rode comfortably in the two-horse trailer swaying gently behind us.

Once we entered Keeneland's sprawling barn area, I spent a few minutes setting up a stall in the barn reserved for ship-ins from other tracks with straw, a water bucket, and some nylon webbing across the door and then unloaded the filly, easing her down the ramp of the trailer and walking her around the ring a few turns to let her stretch her legs. Dan returned from the Racing Secretary's office having placed on file there the filly's registration papers that proved she was a pure Thoroughbred. Jade sat on a bale of straw staring at one of the clearest blue skies I ever remember in my life.

None of this activity was the least bit unusual. He always shipped the stable north after a winter meet at Fairgrounds in New Orleans. But, Dan didn't like moving around so much, an unusual trait considering we were in a business that forced us to live as gypsies. However, for that reason we moved the horses directly into Churchill every spring and trained over their track. From Louisville, Dan picked races that fit an individual horse in his twenty-head stable when Latonia and Keeneland ran their meets during March and April. On the days of those particular races, we simply hooked up his trailer and hauled that horse to its appointment with destiny and pulled it home after the race. Latonia was less than a hundred miles due east and Keeneland less than a hundred miles southeast, an inexpensive drive in the days when gasoline topped out at 44 cents a gallon. Then, when the long meet at Churchill opened in May, we weren't required to move from either of the other tracks. We were already home.

However, on this particular day my boss had decided to include Jade since the new truck had wider seats and she could fit between us easier than in his old half-ton Ford pickup. Jade was a soft-hearted person and talented pony girl but extremely wide. From behind, it was no great shakes to imagine two jiggling hams stuffed in her jeans when she walked. We had been forced to buy a step stool in order to maneuver her up and into the saddle when she rode her pony alongside thoroughbreds to keep them quietly directed during training hours at Churchill. I had great admiration for the stoic resignation of her pinto pony.

Beyond that, she and Dan both drank enough vodka to cancel the Soviet Union's national debt. I didn't mind being around either of them when they drank alone. On this day, they drank together at the bar in the grandstand area. I stayed at the barn grooming the filly for her race. By the fifth race, which was ours, I knew they would be plastered and I would be left to bring the filly to the paddock alone, saddle her, walk her back after the race, bathe her, cool her out, and feed her a few oats before loading up for the return to Louisville.

And, that was exactly what happened. As if my prediction set the event in motion, I found myself alone, after the fifth race, at the receiving barn bathing a sweaty thoroughbred that had just run seventh in a field of nine. Jade and Dan didn't appear over the horizon till the parking lots began to empty and the brilliant gold sun dulled to a dusky red.

Stumbling down the rolling green hill that led from the main track area to the receiving barn, Dan stopped occasionally to lift one leg and then the other and wipe his alligator skin cowboy boots on the back of his one-piece gray leisure suit. He could stand most things in life except dust on the sheen of those boots. Each time he stopped, Jade, who waddled behind his long stride with her tree-trunk legs, caught up and began screaming in his ear. Even though I couldn't hear anything the tone of her voice seemed obvious because her sausage-like finger was wagging in his face vehemently as her lips twisted into a grimace. The people they passed jerked their heads around to stare as if a stabbing had occurred. At each juncture, Dan simply finished wiping his boots, shook his great mane of bushy silver hair, and stepped off. Then, Jade would lean forward and quickstep after him. At one point, I held my breath as she almost toppled head-over-heels and rolled downhill in a huge lard ball. The top of her torso seemed to be outrunning the bottom. Just when I thought she would fall, her bottom half would catch up and start the process over.

Out of breath, they reached me as I finished cooling out the filly by letting her graze on some bluegrass. Jade bent over and grabbed her knees to suck air. Dan lit a Tareyton. Jade straightened up.

"I don't know what the fuck you think you're doing, old man. I saw you patting the waitress on the ass in the clubhouse," she screeched.

"You're dreaming," said Dan.

"The only thing I'm dreaming about is how I'm gonna cut your balls off."

"Help Jim with the filly, you fat hog."

"Fat hog? Fat hog?" Her lower lip began to tremble. She wiped her hands up and down on the pink jumpsuit that stretched across her body. "I bought this new outfit for you, honey. Don't you like it?" Jade squealed. The pink color and the tight fit of the jumpsuit created a second skin that did give her the appearance of a huge freshly weaned shoat. But, I kept my mouth shut even though I could see Dan's point.

"Moo," he said.

"You're such a dumb son-of-a-bitch you don't even know what sound a hog makes," screamed Jade as Dan turned away shaking his head.

He listed left and, limping slightly as he sometimes did when his back bothered him, hobbled off to the parking area to retrieve the truck and trailer. In her customary way of helping me, Jade turned the two five gallon buckets that I had been using to wash the filly with upside down and sat, staring off after her man.

"I just truly don't know what to do. I love him, but he's meaner than a snake when he gets drunk and has no consideration for my feelings. I'm a sensitive person. I ought to just pack up my things and just leave. I could get a job with a dozen different stables around here. What would you do?"

"You're asking the wrong person," I said, and threw a light fly net over the filly so the ugly, blue faced insects couldn't get to her back with their vicious and insatiable appetites. Horse fly bites were non-lethal, but extremely irritating.

"How can you say that? Haven't you been to college?"

I sensed a trap. I had gotten pretty good at recognizing ambushes from the time I spent as a point man with 9th Marines in the jungles of Vietnam and this one was a killer for sure. If I told her to leave, she would get angry because I was trying to break her and Dan up. If I told her to stay, she would get angry because I advocated for his continuing abuse. As I would with any emotionally uncomfortable situation at this time in my life, I simply ignored Jade's questions and tugged the bored race horse around the walking ring a few more turns, stopping every lap by her water bucket to offer her a drink.

***

We were less than fifteen miles from Louisville when Jade started up again. Considering Dan's drunken state, I had asked him to let me drive. He refused. Taking the truck keys from a Kentucky hardboot horse trainer implied you thought him to be less than a man. I was on dangerous ground just bringing the subject up.

Somehow, he was navigating the twilight trip on I-64 without any catastrophic events, as if the new truck had auto pilot instead of cruise control. Leaning against the passenger side door exhausted, I rode with my eyelids drooping, but unable to nap for fear of awakening to a truck and a trailer tumbling end over end down one of the gently rolling hillsides that drooped away from the asphalt.

Both Jade and Dan had begun to suffer physically. They had forgotten the cardinal rule of afternoon drinking – don't stop until you fall asleep at night.

"Why do you always do that every time you drink?" Jade asked.

"Do what?"

"Pretend you don't love me."

"I drink every day."

"You bastard. That slut waitress gave you her phone number. I know she did."

With that indictment, the tormented woman stuck her hand in the side pocket of Dan's leisure suit.

"If I find her number in here, I'll kill you. I'll kill us all."

With her other hand, she grabbed the steering wheel as if to jerk us off the road.

"You crazy bitch," Dan roared and swung his right hand into her face. The backhanded slap splattered against her wide, flat nose pushing it inward and making it wider and flatter for an instant. Blood flew in all directions. Red rain fell on the new dash, my tee-shirt, the windshield, the lapels of Dan's leisure suit, and in color-coordinated freckles across the front of Jade's new pink outfit.

"You broke my nose again." She choked the words out while trying to suck air through her mouth.

"You're breaking my heart with all these accusations," explained Dan matter-of-factly, as if he had just punished a fractious horse.

I wanted to say something profound, utter some wisdom that might help both of them understand that violence should never be associated with love. The idea went against everything humans get taught from the time we're old enough to learn, excluding, of course, the swats I received from my Dad as a disobedient child. He always preceded those beatings with the parental disclaimer – *this will hurt me more than it hurts you*. This was a sure indication that in that instance love and violence were a matched set, like salt and pepper shakers.

My panic overrode my need to be philosophical and, coupled with the knowledge that they had lived together for years in this minefield of a relationship with no thought of separation, I wasted no time trying to examine what kept them together.

"Stop the fucking truck, right now." I said, my voice trembling enough for Dan to sense the mixture of fear and anger. He pulled onto the shoulder of the road and sat head bowed and silent with Jade bleeding beside him. The two of them reminded me of schoolchildren waiting for the teacher to scold them for writing notes to each other during class. The analogy seemed weak considering their argument could have been fatal to us all.

"Sorry," Jade whimpered.

"I'm getting out right here and hitchhiking back to Churchill Downs. If the two of you are lucky enough to make it, I'll see you in the morning at the barn. If you want to kill each other, you'll do it without me."

"Sorry. She just drives me nuts sometimes."

"Yeah, I do," said Jade. "Please don't get out. Who's gonna unload the filly and bed her down?"

"I ride back on one condition. I sit in the middle and you two don't speak," I said to them both.

They agreed. No one spoke until the filly had been returned to her stall in Barn 23 at Churchill Downs. It was past eight p.m. I filled the water buckets in the barn, checking each horse as I did to make sure none had developed colic or become cast against a stall wall. They all seemed healthy and, unlike their human caretakers, emotionally content. Only the sounds of crickets chirping and their own munching of hay interfered with the relaxed silence that coated the indigo night. In the feed shed Dan mixed up a tub full of oats, sweet feed, and vitamins, covered it with bran and then cooked it in boiling water for a few minutes, making what we called hot mash. This was the usual post-race meal. Horses digested the soft mixture easily and it seemed to restore them quicker than dry feed.

Meanwhile, Jade restored herself with a pint bottle of Dark Eyes vodka she happened to find in a medicine chest hanging outside the tack room. Quickly, Dan joined her and soon the bottle was emptied. Still, the only sounds hanging over the barn area were the banging of metal feed tubs against the wooden walls, some satisfied whinnies, and the rustle of dry straw as a horse scratched around sniffing for an unexplored patch on the floor of its twelve foot by twelve foot stall. Out from under the barn roof, stars flashed and shimmied against the sky like sequins on a dark blue cocktail dress. A soft spring breeze carried the scent of honeysuckle and horse manure past my nose.

I was home and safe. The random explosion of violence during the twilight hours unnerved me, not because violence was foreign to my sensibilities but precisely because it wasn't. I should have been far more upset with Dan and Jade's behavior. The fact that their abusive relationship seemed acceptable to me, not necessarily reasonable but tolerable, made me wonder how much of my own humanity had been stripped away by the war. I was home. But, was I really safe?

"I'm hungry," slurred Jade, as she tripped over a rake leaning against the tack room door. "Goddamn it. Who put that there?"

"You did, before we went to Keeneland," Dan said.

"Get me some food," she ordered.

"What's open now?" asked Dan.

"You know what I want."

Jade snuggled against Dan, who had joined her in the doorway of the tack room. She leaned into his ear and whispered something I couldn't hear, but he responded by rubbing his hand up and down between her legs.

"Yeah, I know what you want. So, let's go to White Castle's," he said.

Ordinarily, I would rather have had a root canal than get back into the truck with my boss and his girlfriend, but I hadn't eaten since noon. The track kitchen had long been closed. Dan offered to buy, and a hungry person will take great risks for free food. The half-dollar sized hamburgers, steamed and loaded with onions would hit the spot before settling down for a night's sleep amidst the smell of leather and black strap molasses that had soaked into my cot.

When we arrived at the fine dining establishment, Jade forced us to watch as she ate thirty-six cheeseburgers in the time it took Dan and me to split a dozen. Dan furrowed his brow each time she shoved a whole burger in her mouth. Like shoveling coal into an insatiable locomotive engine, her hand went from bag to the gaping maw in the middle of her chins with a metronomic regularity that astounded me. Dan's face began to redden the tighter he squeezed his brows together. I knew he was trying not to speak for fear his words would initiate another battle. But, I guessed the reason he didn't want another battle had more to do with not killing Jade than with offending her.

After the ground beef carnage, Dan backed the truck out of White Castle and eased down some side street between Southern Parkway and the backside barn area of Churchill Downs. Two blocks later, he pulled to the curb.

"Why are we stopping, honey?" asked Jade.

"No particular reason. Jim, I think my back tire's a little low. Will you get out and check it?"

I felt nothing in our ride that indicated a low tire, but he was the boss. Stepping on the running board, I leaned out and looked toward the front and rear of the truck. Under the street lamp rising from the curb, both tires seemed fully inflated.

"Don't just stand there. Go kick the back tire."

Stepping away from the running board, I walked to the rear of the truck and felt the back tire. It was fine, as I had already indicated. Jade screamed, "No Dan, don't." I rushed back toward the cab in time to see her fly past the open passenger side door. Her huge ass met the street with a sound similar to a bag of sand being tossed onto another bag of sand from a second story window. She grunted. Dan's cowboy boot appeared in the space where Jade had been.

"Get in," he said calmly and pulled me by the collar of my T-shirt.

"What about her?"

"Is she conscious?"

"She looks kind of dazed, but she's sitting up okay in the street."

"Good." As he spoke, Dan reached across me and pulled the cab door shut. "Let's get out of here before she realizes we're gone. I had to kick the fat hog out of the truck before I killed her. She makes me sick."

In the rearview mirror, I saw Jade rise from the asphalt and raise her right arm in a defiant gesture. Her lips moved, and I felt sure she was screaming obscenities, but all I heard was Dan gun the truck motor and tires squealing as we turned the corner.

"You can't leave her," I said, half concerned about Jade's welfare and half-panicked for any good Samaritan passing by who might mistake her for a human being in need.

"It's the only way I can get rid of her."

"Do you really want to get rid of her, Dan?"

The question seemed to startle him. Easing the truck to a curb, he put it into park and looked at me with an expression of confusion like a child who has just watched his dog get struck by a car.

"Sometimes I do because I can't stand being around her. Other times, she'll do something really nice for me like go get the Racing Form early on Sunday morning and bring it back with some Dunkin' Donuts. Then, I think I might really love her. I'm just tired of her whining and eating all the time."

"We still can't leave her alone in this neighborhood. She could get mugged, or hit by a car, and then you'd feel like shit in the morning."

"You're right. But I don't want to sleep with her in our apartment. This is our breakup. I'm done with her. I'll give her some money in the morning and send her on her way. I know a cheap motel out on Dixie Highway. We can get separate rooms for the night. I'll do it if you stay in my room with me. I don't want her trying to wake me up all night to satisfy her carnal desires. She'll leave me alone if you're with me."

The rest of the night in a sleazy motel with two volatile drunks seemed less preferable than open heart surgery without anesthesia. On the other hand, what little conscience I had brought home from the war refused to allow me abandoning any woman, even Jade, on a street in a rough neighborhood, especially since she may have been injured in the fall from Dan's new truck. By midnight the three of us settled into two motel rooms. Jade, crying and complaining that her tailbone might be broken, closed her door. Dan and I sat up on our respective beds in the adjoining double room until I fell back into a dreamless sleep.

In the morning, a knock on the door awakened me. I opened it to find Dan and Jade standing together arm in arm with hot coffee for me.

"I couldn't sleep so I went next door to apologize to Jade…"

"And before you know it he had my panties off and was riding me like the little stallion I remember from when we first met five years ago. He was just full of hot desire and I couldn't resist."

I worked another few months for Dan after that spring night, and then left to start my own horse training business in the winter of 1976. The man taught me an incredible amount about conditioning thoroughbred race horses and I operated a successful public stable for several years. On the other hand, I'm still trying to discern if he taught me anything useful about the nature of human desire. I do know that when I left his employment, he and Jade had just gotten engaged.

Chapter Twelve

The Question of Balance

Having been indoctrinated into the cult of manliness by John Bill McGarrah during a league bowling night in 1960, I felt ready to handle any obstacle that might be placed before me on the path to adulthood. In the men's room of the bowling alley, a strange contraption hung above a row of porcelain urinals. If you put in a quarter, the machine claimed to spit out a small foil package containing a condom. Supposedly this device prevented disease and in a bowling alley restroom I could understand why that might have been a major concern. Terrified, I asked my father what was safe to touch.

"What the hell are you babbling about, boy," he said.

"Disease, disease. I don't want to catch anything and die." I answered and pointed to the machine on the wall.

"You won't catch *that* kind of problem on a toilet seat or anywhere else in here. Men have tried to use that excuse for years and it just won't fly."

Confused, I asked him to buy one just in case. He laughed.

"Look, this thing is what we men call a cut rubber. It's like a balloon only you don't blow it up. You put it on your pecker before you screw a woman, if you ever happen to be lucky enough to screw one."

"Why?" I said.

"Women sometimes have germs that make your pecker burn

when you pee. Now, I've told you all you need to know. I'm trying to bowl a 200 average for the night, don't bother me with questions. As ugly as you are, this conversation will probably be as close to using one as you ever get."

Certainly, this was as close as my father and I came to having a discussion about dating and how a man might learn to pursue a relationship with a woman. My mother, on the other hand, felt differently about my prospects and my need for education in the not-so-subtle art of conquest. Yes, I said conquest. Mom learned gender roles in the 1950's when feminism meant soft skin and crocodile tears, long before it could be considered a movement toward equality. Men were dominant and women were submissive. It was the hunter/gatherer Eisenhower era. It was understood by almost everyone. Nature desired each male and female to adhere to their natural, albeit unfair, roles.

However, mom believed also that any twelve year old male who aspired to success in his endeavors might someday require more than a cursory knowledge of the condom-on-penis conundrum as well. Women respected men who were civilized when performing their god-given duties as rulers. To that end, she enrolled me in Mrs. Kendall's ballroom dancing class. This class, which the mortician's wife Betty Kendall taught in the living room of their home, took place every Thursday after school on south Main Street in our little farm community of Princeton, Indiana. Connected to the makeshift dance floor by virtue of a single door was an adjoining room where dead people lived.

The fact that embalming went on a few feet from us as the record player whirred out sounds of "The Tennessee Waltz" cast a pall of eerie claustrophobia, like a wet wool blanket, over the airy space cleared of furniture each week. When added to the eclectic blend of shy, male little league ball players, confused female junior high school debutantes, and Betty's bizarre appearance – a kaleidoscopic melting of purple eye shadow into black mascara into ruby red lipstick and orange foundation – the surrealistic atmosphere of my new reality generated a recalcitrant outbreak of acne, sweaty palms, and nausea every time I entered the brick building. As I look back on it now, the close presence of girls may have influenced my complexion too, along with new surges of testosterone that often left my stomach feeling like I had ridden fast over a steep hill in the back seat of dad's Desoto.

I stepped on Susan's toes every time we tried to waltz and Judy laughed each time Mike or Barry bumped into Mrs. Kendall's coffee table or tripped over a lamp cord. Still, I survived the first two weeks of the waltz, the cha-cha, and the foxtrot fairly well. It seemed as if I might actually become a gentleman after all in harmony with my mother's dream. Then, Denise showed up for our third session. Every anxiety any psychologist had ever imagined wormed its way into my rattled psyche upon the arrival of my seventh-grade goddess. My new red corduroy trousers looked stupid. My shoes lacked polish and white socks were uncool. The purple polyester shirt I got for Christmas from my aunt was showing rings of sweat under my arms. I should have applied more English Leather and made my father teach me to shave. During the first cha-cha, I lost my balance three times, tripping over my own feet and falling into Susan's perky breasts. On the third trip, I saw Denise smile at me as she glided swan-like across the floor, her hand in Mike's hand. My cheeks flushed. I could never raise my head and stare into those beautiful blue eyes again. My mother had ruined my life.

Then, our dance instructor, frustrated with the incompetence she was forced to witness, thought a change of pace might do us all some good and decided to let us practice more contemporary movements, undulations each of us had grown familiar with thanks to Dick Clark's American Bandstand and Chubby Checker. That's when the beast was born. Judy called lady's choice and now that there were three boys and three girls, Mrs. Kendall could rest from Barry's toe-tapping assaults. Denise chose me. My knees buckled when she pointed her elegant finger as sure as if it had been a gun aimed and fired point blank at my heart.

White socks slipped and slid across the floor, buffing the varnished wood to the rhythmic angst of The Jarmels – *A little bit of soap will wash away your lipstick from my face, but a little bit of soap will never nevernevernever erase, the pain in heart and my eyes as I go through the lonely years, a little bit of soap will never wash away my tears.*

We swirled and bounced, shifting from foot to foot, dodging the collective smell of Clearasil and English leather, ignoring the tragic reality of the lyrics. Denise arched her back, and stretched her perfect little breasts against her black sweater. Those nipples made me dream about being a hunger that she might dream about. Her small hands replaced the neck of a *Louisville Slugger* in my sweaty palms and we danced, not just the Twist, the Mashed Potato, the Swim, and the Bristol Stomp, but something greater, more intricate than the footwork, wilder than the 2-4 drumbeat. We danced till we became the dance, as if the rhythm remolded us into strange new creatures whose only desire was to feel the blood boil and rise in our veins, then fade while Mrs. Kendall changed the record and then rise again with a new urgency created by Berry Gordy and his repetition of language and rhythm and melody.

> *Do you love me, I can really move*
> *Do you love me, I'm in the grove*
> *Do you love me, nnnooown*
> *That I can dance. Do you Do you Do you*
> *Do you love me, now that I can dance.*

All too soon the brief respite ended. I returned to the iambic pentameter of a waltz and the self-consciousness generated by the discipline of form, grace and the intimacy of close bodily contact. I'd like to report that Mrs. Kendall's six-week ballroom dancing class made me a civilized gentleman. Unfortunately, my mother was proven wrong. I have remained clumsy and out of balance around women. Never quite able to adjust when the feminist movement took hold, I continued opening doors and giving my seat away on the bus even when chastised for being condescending. Once, I suffered the indignity of an harassment complaint for mentioning to a co-worker that I liked her dress. During the evolution of the sensitive man in the 21st century, I have been unable to believe that my wife's monthly desire for chocolate has nothing to do with PMS, *really*. I will never accept that the cult of Oprah is open to males, or that women come from Venus while men come from Mars. Denise has married someone else, twice.

As for dancing, I quit altogether after I saw *Saturday Night Fever* in 1977. The idea that I would have to trade my levis and tie-dyed tee shirts in for a three piece white suit coupled with the fact that cover bands had replaced the Rolling Stones' earthy tones with a sort of squealing Bee Gees mimesis terrified me to such an extent that I could no longer spend evenings in my favorite night clubs.

Throughout my life balance in all things great and small has been what I have needed most. When I struggle and gain it, I'm forced to struggle even harder to maintain it. Maybe that's just the way we all live, stumbling back and forth, caught in the ever-shrinking space that separates life from death. Some days I wake up to the waltz and other days, the twist. Most days I find myself balanced somewhere between Tchaikovsky and Chubby Checker, between the smell of lilacs leaking through the walls from the last funeral and the flush of blood rising with Denise's touch, between the need for stability and the desire for excess. But, it isn't such a bad place to be when you consider that the alternative to the struggle for balance awaits us all in that *other* room right off the dance floor.

***

A successful horse trainer learns early in his career that balance is a quality hard to achieve, difficult to maintain, but necessary for survival. He serves as caretaker for expensive thoroughbreds twenty-four hours a day, seven days a week. Not only does he feed, exercise, medicate, and placate their bodies and temperaments, he acts much like an agent for any stable of professional athletes coordinating races and training procedures and conducting business with their owners while attempting to hustle new clients. Beyond all of this, some equilibrium as a human is required, especially if the trainer has a family or desires sanity. Fortunately for me, my mother forced me to begin the constant struggle for balance at an early age and the concept has remained a guiding principle throughout my life.

This was the limbo I had reached on the racetrack: floating somewhere between Barry's lack of balance in the business of winning races and Dan's lack of concern about the minute details of caring for thoroughbreds when they were off the track and housed in a stall. I had learned an incredible amount about both aspects of being a trainer and felt ready to dance successfully balanced between the two. John Bill and I spoke of these matters in the track kitchen one morning early in the November race meet at Churchill Downs. He agreed that I should take my trainer's exam and if I passed, become sole caretaker of our three horses. From there, it would be up to me to build my stable with other clients over time. We started from the same reasoning point, more control over our own horses. As usual problems developed. I meant a bigger voice for me in future endeavors, and he meant a bigger voice for him. Things were still a little out of balance.

Chapter Thirteen

Out of Focus

I grew up thinking that all good men gambled. It was just the way things were. My close association with gambling on everything, including race horses, came long before computers compiled the line from Vegas or satellites carried major sports on closed circuit TV thanks to the Palace Pool Room. On the weekends, my old man sat me by a radio that housed flowing tubes of light. Those tubes produced sound from their brightness, a sort of Motorola synesthesia. Magically, the screeching, hissing, static would sometimes form actual words – Hodges…swings…back…against…wall. It's gone…Dodgers…two runs…two hits…no errors – as I leaned into the noise to concentrate. More wondrous than the talking box was the ticker tape machine that rose next to it from a rickety table with uneven legs. It seemed a simple enough device, a few small gears and a tiny roll of paper on a metal spindle beneath a glass dome. Yet at the end of each inning of every major league baseball game being played on any particular day during the summer, the gears rattled and hummed, turning paper through an ink-fed punch. The clacking sound reminded me of Southern Freight trains pounding over loose tracks at the Hall Street crossing by Lowell Elementary School.

As the ribbon of paper tracked through a slight opening near the bottom of the glass globe someone sitting nearby tore it off, stretched it out arm's length, and read off the ball scores from around the country that had been etched into the white surface with black ink. Over the clang and thump of nearby pinball machines, whoever confiscated the enchanted strip screamed out the numbers and the names – "Cardinals 4, Dodgers 6, 5th inning." "Yankees 2, Red Sox

Nothing, 8th inning" – like a sideshow barker at the county fair. Depending on who had money placed where, these reports were often followed by words my father never allowed me to say, especially around my mother.

One more sound always completed the cycle every fifteen or twenty minutes. A small man with a shaved head and a toothless grin scratched the information across a screeching chalkboard. His name was George and he had been orphaned as a young child. George fit the description of what we now call a developmentally disabled person. Back then, people had less sensitive language to use. We labeled him our local retarded guy because he could barely read and seemed happy working for tips.

George wasn't always treated with kindness by the clientele, me included as I grew into a teenager. But he also wasn't nearly as dumb as we believed. A couple of older kids had given George a lit cherry bomb when he was very small and called it candy. The firecracker exploded in his mouth and his face took on a sad, twisted, grimace afterwards that was enhanced by his lack of teeth and his slovenly speech patterns. Big Jim, who owned the pool room, helped George save his tip money in the bank and rented him a room at the Emerson Hotel. Because of Jim's generosity and guidance George managed to save a good sum of money and live a fairly comfortable life for many years. As time went by, the man became an icon and probably more recognizable in the tri-state area than the town mayor. Even George's eventual downfall remains the stuff of legend. Unknown to Big Jim, he withdrew his savings, took a bus to St. Louis and hired a hooker for a night. The adventure ruined George in many ways and he ended up in the county home for indigents. That's a story for another time.

Baseball was hardly the only thing you could bet on. In those Eisenhower days after WWII, the white men folk of rural Southern Indiana felt confident and prosperous enough to bet on anything. Most of them had been through the horrific experience of a war and, as odd as it may seem, gambling replaced that need for an adrenalin rush with far less risk. One day, during the summer of the same year I got my basketball goal hung in Dad's auto garage, George Land, a notorious liar who stuttered when he lied, sat on a bench by the ticker tape machine. He said, "It is so hot today that I'll bbbbbe dddddamned if I dddidn't fry eggs and bbacon on the sidewalk in front of my house this mmmmorning, just to save a little on my utttility bbill."

The Cardinals were losing and Mr. Archer, who always bet on them, spit a stream of tobacco toward the brass spittoon with a sigh.

"You're a fucking liar," said Doodlebug Rainey while playing a game of snooker.

"I cccan prove it"

"I got ten bucks says you can't."

By now, the entire room had gone quiet. A challenge had been offered and money was on the line. Some men reached into their pockets wanting to sweeten the pot, but mostly no one was willing to bet against Doodlebug who won his wagers frequently. Through the blue cigar smoke, above the hum of the ceiling fan, over an occasional nervous cough, and beyond the scent of cooking onions, the voice of authority boomed. "I'll back Doodlebug, but only 3 to 2." Big Jim, the owner of the establishment had offered to book all bets on Doodlebug but at the payoff rate of one dollar for every two dollars someone wagered. It seemed like a good investment to most of the guys. As matter of fact it seemed like a sure thing. Concrete was porous and could never heat up enough to fry the egg.

On the other hand, Big Jim was not a gambler. He made book and that was business. Jim never did anything stupid. If he thought George had no shot at winning, he would never have taken any money at all. The gambling fever rose to a frenzy and some of the old boys figured Jim knew some egg-frying science that they weren't aware of and planned to cash in on his secret knowledge. Money started coming in on both sides now, which had been the plan all along. With enough money bet both ways, Jim could pay off either side, keep his house cut of 20% and end up making a clear profit no matter what happened.

When the furor subsided, the short order cook behind the counter handed George an unbroken egg. Doodlebug said, "Prove your point, or not" and out the door they went, followed by the entire crowd, about ten men in all. Women weren't allowed in the pool rooms in those days before Gloria Steinem and Cosmopolitan magazine. The crowd on the sidewalk drew the attention of others around the town square. I saw clerks from the courthouse across the street crowd against the windows, their curiosity overwhelming their work ethic. Shoppers strolled out of the Ben Franklin Five & Dime store and peered at the large circle of sweating men. Greek's Candy Store emptied its tables and soda fountain stools as the loafers in there followed the commotion.

George Land stepped ceremoniously to the center, kneeled, and cracked the egg on the curb. Splitting the shell apart slowly, he let the egg white drip out onto the hot concrete until the yolk squeezed out whole and plopped in the center of the puddle. At first nothing happened. The circle tightened and everyone leaned in. Someone threw an elbow into Bill Wheeler's ribs jostling for a better position. Doodlebug got down on his hand and knees next to George. With his face almost flush on the sidewalk, he stared at the edges of the egg puddle. I did too, and I swear the borders of that egg began turning white like you might see one do in a skillet that was just heating up. But before it could be called one way or the other, one of Roy Swain's mangy old dogs crept into the circle as if it was a henhouse and sucked that egg, yolk and all, down his gullet and then licked the sidewalk clean. Roy, who had no interest in the doings of other humans, whistled and the dog rejoined the pack, which disappeared around the corner. A collective groan and cries of "foul" "unfair" "redo" echoed around the circle.

Everyone who reads this and lived in Princeton at the time will remember that story differently, especially if that reader happens to be male and hung around the pool room in the late nineteen-fifties. It quickly became legend and every legend has many versions. This, however, is my story. If you think of the scene as happening some other way, write your own fucking story. The point is simple; gambling thrived as an illegal form of entertainment even though frowned upon by the righteous. It provided a necessary form of release from the monotony of life in those days. What got frowned on in public often got accepted with quiet acquiescence in private, like drinking during the Prohibition Era. That's just the way things were, and the Palace held an honored place as the center of that nefarious enterprise in all of Gibson County.

The county elected a new prosecuting attorney every few years. The lawyers always swore by all that was holy to stamp out bookmaking and pinball playing at the Palace. They made these blood oaths, like Eliot Ness, at every church ice cream social, PTA meeting, and Rotary Club breakfast for weeks before the elections. The week after the election, the pool room regulars could count on a dramatic raid. This became sacrosanct for a newly elected prosecutor after Robert Stack came on TV starring in the *Untouchables*. We were never disappointed. Ironically, once the Princeton Daily Clarion carried the front page story of the raid complete with pictures, the prosecutors always found themselves back in the pool room a week or so later to eat an egg sandwich and check the morning line on the Cardinals game. It was just the way things were. If you've been paying attention to Congress lately, you'll realize that most people never question the ethics of behavior that is attached to the movement of money, especially if they stand a chance of getting some.

I didn't know it at the time I left Dan's employment and struck out on my own, but the whole capitalistic enterprise that makes America be America had begun to travel backwards, as well. I began my own small business with great hope for success at a time in America when small businesses were starting to lose the ability to be successful.

Like the great Robber Barons of the Industrial Revolution that crushed competitors, rigged markets, and corrupted governments, huge corporations were taking over every aspect of American life, farming, oil, education, industry, even horse breeding and racing. Their bottom-line purpose for existence as corporate entities was and remains maximizing shareholder profit. In their greed and power, they disrupted the American Dream and destroyed the notion that a little mom & pop operation could compete with them on almost any level. Everything was moving in one direction, the disassembly of democracy as a way of life and its replacement with capitalism. What used to be two good and worthy principles working together now moved in the direction of mutual exclusivity. In other words, money talked and bull shit walked.

Sure, purse money has grown exponentially at small tracks since I raced horses thirty some years ago. Backside barn areas have been renovated, dorms erected for the comfort of stable hands, and tracks like Ellis Park in the Midwest that have survived give away over a million bucks in stakes money each year. They draw better horses and more famous riders. People are willing to bet more when they see a better show. It all sounds good, but these factors actually make life difficult, if not impossible, for the small-time operator. I'm sure people who own independent stores struggle with big corporate competitors, like Wal-Mart or Target. But, that struggle can assume epic proportions at a bush league racetrack. If you don't win races, you don't eat and neither do the horses.

This system always worked well because trainers who had access to wealthy clients and expensive horses traditionally stayed where the big money is. Then simulcast racing came about. The ability to legally open a track grandstand and take bets from all the major tracks racing year-round allowed the little places a much larger income, and consequently they increased the purse structure during racing season. Suddenly, big operators such as oil-rich sheiks from the Middle East, syndicates of doctors and lawyers, Wall Street holding companies, movie stars, and national celebrities that once used horse racing as a tax shelter smelled easy money and ordered their trainers to ship their well-bred horses to cheap tracks. The racing program was flooded with more competition than the little guys could stand. Their own cheaper, slower horses lost races that, under ordinary circumstances, they could win. Small-time operators went broke. While purses continue to grow, the fields of horses in each race during racing season lessen, and the quality of the horses running diminishes.

When any community sacrifices its values and traditions motivated by greed alone, it runs the risk of losing its identity.

The dedication and work ethic shown by these small-time stable owners is difficult to discover in the modern, profit motivated, business of racing. The form of the sport remains. Horses run around a dirt track from a starting gate to a wire. Spectators bet on the order of finish. But, the substance is gone. Horseracing has become all about money. The glory is fading. The thrill of competing is being reduced by the anxiety of earning. Most of the old indigent and itinerant Hard Boots have either died or gone to pasture at county rest homes, replaced by vacant eyed runaways and illegal aliens who work twelve hours a day without any soul. These people also work without developing a rhythm of life. The horses in their care are dumb animals to be exploited, as they themselves are dumb animals to be exploited. It's a job and nothing more.

There was a need for Ellis Park and many other small racing facilities across this country to expand their economic base of operations. Any business has to increase its income in direct proportion to the increase in overhead. But, that's a fiscal concern. It doesn't have to be the only concern. A wealth of emotion and energy, a time-honored tradition of sportsmanship, a way of life began to disappear because of this over-emphasis on profit at all cost.

Beyond what was happening on a grand, historical scale to the whole country, the very first winter on my own was one of the worst in Kentucky history. As an unknown trainer with untried horses, I had neither the political or economic pull to demand stalls at crowded racetracks during the meet days. In December of 1976 I rented three stalls at a place called The Kentucky Training Center on Paris Pike just outside of Lexington, Kentucky, and shipped my father's horses there. The training center resembled a federal prison, whitewashed, concrete block buildings with rows of tiny stalls covered by metal bars. There were no windows, only sterile fluorescent lights that hung like dying stars from metal rafters high above the dirt floor. A small tunnel led outside to a covered five-furlong track of clay and sand. The sunlight available was in the thirty minute period when you and your horse might venture to the track for exercise, as a prisoner might walk the yard, and even then the track was covered by a tin roof.

By January of 1977 temperatures had reached minus sixteen degrees Fahrenheit, unheard of in this region of the country. The training center became an ice box. Every hour on the hour for days, I had to break the ice in the plastic water buckets and add hot water so my charges could drink. One morning after finishing the daily ritual of feeding oats, cleaning stalls, exercising horses, and breaking ice in water buckets – I don't remember what day of the week it was because the days all bled into each other with a never-ending routine and constant fear of frostbite – a small group of hearty souls gathered around a kerosene space heater. As we huddled in a tight circle of heavy parkas and leather gloves, I remember asking someone what the temperature was.

"It's eight," she replied.

"Eight above or eight below?" I asked

"When it's eight, what does it matter whether it's above or below? You just suffer through and do your job."

That stoicism along with the self-discipline I had learned from my time in the Marine Corps got me through the winter. Of course, it helped that the horses remained healthy and seemed to enjoy the frigid atmosphere and that the girl who answered my question had rented a small cabin directly across the road from the training center with a pot belly stove and a huge bed.

With spring and better weather, my sprits improved. The horses trained well and Huffy Lady, along with Sanden King began earning purse money. By paying their way and a little more, the horses allowed us to expand the business. My father proved to be very adept at judging a thoroughbred's potential through research, especially in the Daily Racing Form. He would call before post time on a given race day at one track or another and say something on the order of, "I put some money in my account. Try to get a look at the number four horse in the sixth race before he runs. If he looks sound or you can work with him, claim him."

Claiming was a form of gambling in a big way. It allowed people to buy horses that are fit and running. If you entered a horse in this type of race at a predetermined purchase price, which ran the gamut from $1500 at some tracks to $100,000 at others, then that horse could be bought up until the last second before the starting gate opened and the race began.

The rules were simple and brutal. The horse was running for its previous owner but when the race began, it ran for you. Confusing? Not really. In other words, if it placed in the race and earned any purse money that prize went to the other fellow. If the horse won, he could not take it back. If it fell over dead coming out of the starting gate, you bought it. Still, this was the cheapest way to get into the race horse game. My father was a good salesmen and he pitched a pretty good line to several of his wealthier friends. They all loved to bet and they all loved the prestige of being in racing. The "sport of kings" made them feel like royalty. Most people need more than money to feel rich. These clients were businessmen who wanted to own a horse as a hobby or as a tax write-off and most didn't want to invest more than a few thousand dollars initially. You could claim a horse already racing rather than buy one a year or two old and then pay for breaking it, training it to run on a track, and boarding for a year or more while you hoped it remained sound without an injury that would sabotage a career as yet not started. My father learned the hard way with the purchase of Sanden King, Huffy Lady, and Jim's Jungle Joy. The first two paid their way but the last one never won a race. Consequently, most of the horses I trained were purchased for him and my other clients over the years by claim. More often than not, my father's claiming advice proved profitable as far as paying the way for a small stable like mine.

I won a lot of races over the next few years with claimed horses at Churchill Downs, Ellis Park, Hawthorne, Oaklawn, Fairgrounds, Latonia, and Keeneland. I got to travel like a gypsy – Louisville, Chicago, Hot Springs, New Orleans – on the move every few months to complete this yearly circuit of racing. But the business, while allowing much horizontal movement, restricted by its nature any vertical movement. A legendary horse trainer, Sonny Jim Fitzsimmons once quipped, "Trainers don't make horses, horses make trainers." I needed a horse capable of winning high-powered races at big league race tracks in order to attract the attention of wealthy clients looking to purchase and race expensive thoroughbreds. In 1978, I almost made it. Through my father's keen eye and the business sense of three of his close friends, I was given the privilege of training a freak.

Chapter Fourteen

The Storm

The word freak as I used it implies only magical things in this instance. A creature was born and grew to maturity well beyond the ordinary boundaries of his genetics. His mother gave birth in a field after being accidently impregnated by a cheap stallion that jumped a pasture fence the year before. His credentials were so vague and meager as to give the Jockey Club pause before allowing him registration as a full-bloodied thoroughbred in order to be eligible for racing. His owner named him Storm Strike and had no idea of his potential, only that he could run faster than the other claiming horses in the stable.

The Oxford dictionary defines magic as having or using special powers to make impossible things happen. This explained Storm Strike. He ran erratically and finished badly in his maiden race at Churchill Downs. His owner/trainer believed the stallion to be outclassed. He brought him home to Ellis Park and had the local veterinarian castrate the animal. Most men will agree that this should have made the horse docile, as it would any male deprived of testosterone. Instead, it created a monster beyond the comprehension of the man who owned him. Storm filled out and grew to a height of seventeen hands. Weighing almost twelve hundred pounds and with a stride double that of most other horses, the newly created gelding ran away from a field of 7500 dollar claimers in his very next race.

When my father saw the horse run and not get claimed, he asked his owner what would buy the three year old. They settled on thirty thousand dollars, a fortune for my father. Consequently, he put together a syndicate of sorts in the early days before syndicates became popular. Three of his close friends chipped in seventy-five hundred dollars apiece and the four of them made the buy. If you follow horse racing you may not remember my dad, Bill Wheeler, or Jim Pegram, but you should know Jim's son, Mike. In this 21st century, Mike Pegram has become one of the preeminent owners in thoroughbred horse racing. His horses have won almost every major stakes race in the country, including the Kentucky Derby and the Preakness in 1998. The horse, named Real Quiet, was beaten by a nose in the Belmont for the Triple Crown. Mike won an Eclipse Award himself on more than one occasion. I'm giving Mike a nod here not because of his success on a path that began in 1978. Other people become wealthy and successful in business all the time. I'm acknowledging a friend who put aside his considerable business interests and flew back home to act as a pall bearer at my father's funeral in 1998.

As for Storm Strike, I led him back to my barn at Ellis Park and within the next six weeks won four major allowance races in a row before Storm Strike threw a bad race and lost the Governor's Handicap at the end of the meet. After resting a month, I shipped him to a small track in Ohio where he ran 1 and 1/16 miles in less than one minute and forty-two seconds breaking the old track record that had stood for decades. This would be classified as magical by my father. Certainly, it was the most fun I had since returning from Vietnam. But as I had learned in 'Nam, magic or what Marines used to call *The Luck* is not real. It is the manifestation of random circumstance that imagination molds into an enchanted narrative. It appears to be with you awhile so you can explain events that should have killed you but killed someone else instead. Then, it drifts on to someone else because you are dead. Fickle, like an Indiana thunderstorm or adolescent love, it materializes from somewhere invisible, graces you with power and elegance and disappears without consulting you or considering your needs.

In the winter between his successful three year old racing season and the beginning of his four year old one, Storm Strike suffered a serious training accident on a sloppy track at Oaklawn Park in Hot Springs, Arkansas. Two small bones commonly called "wing" bones curve up and off of the large coffin bone at the rear in a horse's foot. A sloppy track is wet on the top and like concrete underneath. The soil meant to be a cushion is reduced by rain to muddy soup. In preparing for the Rebel Stakes, my big horse worked four furlongs in 48.1 seconds, way too fast for the track conditions. The rider could not contain the horse's pent up energy. I have no idea at what point the stress fracture occurred, but Storm Strike returned to the barn with a crack in one of those wing bones. Injuries of this type gave rise to the old hardboot saying "no foot, no horse." Because the animal stands so much of every day, foot and leg injuries heal very slowly, sometimes not at all. Storm recovered with time and treatment and late in his four year old season went on to win a few more races, but the gelding never returned to earlier form. Where did the "luck" go? It settled on some other horse in some other racing stable, I guess. Where will the magic go? I have no idea. I am simply happy to have had my dad believe it settled on him. His one desire as a lover of horse racing was to "catch lightning in a bottle," and for an instant, he did.

Left to my own devices I would have never worked Storm Strike on that bad track at Oaklawn Park, Dad and I bickered over the timing and weather for an hour by telephone that morning. In the end, we both bear responsibility for the big horse's injury. I gave in to his reasoning because I wanted him to approve of me more than I wanted to win the quarrel.

The anecdote described on the next few pages has nothing to do with horses but illustrates, dear readers, a huge difference in the way my father and I viewed the world. I have spent much of my adult life attempting to attach meaning to what I witness, to understand some layered resonance in the random events of life, to formulate meaningful substance from a series of simple decisions people make on a daily basis. This has allowed me to generate a shield around my psyche, one that meant my life was in my control. John Bill would have seen this following chapter as a story of good luck, told me to enjoy it, and quit overthinking the banality of life. When luck has chosen you, you're protected. If you don't respect it, you will suffer the wrath of a force beyond your power. These opposing ways of understanding our own realities generated many arguments between us.

Oh, I don't mean that I've never engaged in superstitious behavior. You can't go into something like combat without carrying a talisman – rabbit's foot, girlfriend's garter, Gideon Bible, favorite Zippo – as good luck. It's one way to create the illusion of hope where there is only hopelessness. Everyone does it. But, it's a ritual of form that lacks substance for most of us, something we go through just in case. I have never backed eleven miles down a gravel road in rural Indiana to avoid crossing the path of a black cat, as my father did once. Simply put, he trusted an energy at play in his life beyond his comprehension and I have always been terrified of that possibility. However, as I approach my golden years less than gracefully the greater my tolerance for uncertainty becomes and the more my mind opens to mystery.

Chapter Fifteen

A Matter of Good Luck? You Decide

I saw the Doors unintentionally as a young man. At least, I want to believe it was the Doors. The year was 1967, late summer, and after flunking out of college in my freshman year, I managed to graduate from boot camp at Parris Island, spend two weeks at home on leave without getting laid, and another four weeks of advanced infantry training (AIT) at Camp Lejeune in the woods of North Carolina. Hoping that training was over and ready to get on with the carnage – a stupidly surreal attitude that coincided with the celluloid reality of John Wayne in my youth – I awaited my orders. They came. In its infinite wisdom, Mother Green had decided that all of my training might not be enough if I were captured rather than killed by the Viet Cong.

Consequently, on my way to Vietnam as an 0311 infantry man I joined my fellow replacement troops as part of Third Battalion, 9[Th] Marine Regiment at a stopover just outside San Diego on the west coast – Camp Pendleton. Here, I was instructed in a very basic and brief SERE (survival, escape, resistance, and evasion) course. It seemed useless to me.

We were destined for a miserable hunk of mountain known as the Rock Pile and our mission was to fight the enemy coming across the DMZ till we died. In fact, all of us shipping out of Pendleton would replace Marines who had done just that. The possibility of surrender and capture followed by escape and evasion seemed absurd. Nonetheless, I had never been to California. As a small town boy from the rural Midwest, I relished the idea of seeing somewhere new and held onto that notion to deal with the boredom of more training.

Four weeks of completed training later, I received a weekend pass courtesy of the First Sergeant before shipping out of "the world" and into the combat zone. The sergeant appreciated my phony-brave manner during fake torture by fake Viet Cong after I was fake captured the last few days of SERE. Another Pfc. whose name completely escapes me – let's call him Chuck – had been given a similar pass. He happened to be from Anaheim, a suburb of Los Angeles, and he asked me if I wanted to join him in an adventure before becoming a walking corpse, a *di bo chet*, in the jungles of Southeast Asia. My pockets bulged with all ninety-three dollars from our last pay as we had no way to spend it in the mountains of southern California and I had nowhere else to go.

"What's this great adventure?" I asked.

"Does it matter if I tell you I'm meeting my fiancé and she's bringing her best friend along for you to spend the day with?"

"Is her best friend a breathing female?"

"Yeah, and not bad to look at, except her tits are kind of small," said Chuck.

"More than a mouthful is wasted, my man."

"How would you know?" He asked, lighting a Marlboro.

***

The offer was too enticing to refuse. It wasn't that I missed having sex. Certainly, my experience in a small country high school in Southern Indiana was hands on, but they were mostly my own hands on my own pecker. I felt lonely having no females to talk with for months and the only way to admit that without sounding like a girl myself was to feign the role of deprived stud. Unless, you happen to be a reader raised in the 1950's and 1960's, you may fail to understand the insane homophobia that gripped the military by the balls in those days and grasp how important it was to convince your friends of your manly sexual prowess, especially if you showered with them on a daily basis.

After picking us up at the back gate, his fiancé and her friend treated us to a day at Disneyland, the original one envisioned and built by Walt Disney himself. It was a chance to visit my boyhood heroes Davy Crockett, Zorro, and Texas John Slaughter in Frontier Land. We went to a place called the Space Mountain as well.

True to Chuck's description the girl I had been given as a

going away present – attitudes recorded here predate a feminine sensitivity – was cute in an androgynous, Audrey Hepburn kind of way and her name was Summer, which seemed perfect for a California girl living in what historians now call 1967 – The Summer of Love. She played to Audrey's look by keeping her hair trimmed in a short pixie cut and dyed black. Her bright red lipstick highlighted the almost translucent pearl skin on her cheeks. When she spoke, which was rarely, the words floated out in a soft whisper as if she were terrified of awakening the large animal inside me. Maybe she was. Who knew what she'd been told about Marines on the way to gladiatorial death? She may have been thinking of Eleanor Roosevelt's famous description of us as "over-sexed, under-paid, teenaged killers." I may not have fit her image of ideal companion any more than she fulfilled my busty Farrah Fawcett fantasies. Whatever went on in her head, she was pleasant enough and seemed to tolerate my company as long as I kept my hands to myself and refrained from blurting out motherfucker this and motherfucker that loudly enough to chase away the small children hanging around Frontier Land.

By the time we finished dinner at one of the dozen or so nondescript Mexican restaurants in the Anaheim neighborhood and visited several local night spots familiar to Chuck and Rosalie, midnight had evolved into early morning. My friend and his fiancé began looking for ways to escape us. Each wanted to give the other one of those intense I-may-never-see-you-again fucks that they had witnessed in dozens of bad romantic movies over a short lifetime. On the other hand, I realized early in the evening that Summer had no intention of parting her legs for me. She recoiled quickly from several attempts I made at physical contact, a hand on the bare knee, an arm around the shoulders. Although I felt as if I were being rejected like a hideous troll, she simply exercised caution with her emotions. We barely knew each other's names and I would disappear from her life before sunrise. Realizing her reticence now after forty years makes me aware of how stupidly and unaware young men in heat often behave.

Regardless of the fact that I would not get laid, I had no desire for the night to end considering what awaited me was a bus ride back to Pendleton, a barracks full of sweaty marines, and eventual confrontation with mortality in Southeast Asia. In the pre-dawn of southern California, the sky opened above us into an infinite universe of stars. The streets were lined with palm trees and a warm breeze carried the scent of suntan lotion and jasmine across the asphalt parking lots and concrete sidewalks. My date was pleasant to look at and didn't seem to mind silence broken only by the hiss of an occasional car passing or my awkward company as we strolled along the nearly deserted boulevards of Anaheim.

When our companions drifted away finally toward a cheap motel, Summer and I searched the side streets till we chanced across a small building in a dimly-lit alley referred to in those days as an "after-hours" club, a place to go when you weren't done drinking but the law had forced the nightclubs and bars to quit selling alcohol. The door appeared as an entrance to an ordinary home in the quiet neighborhood and there were no indications other than a small sign on the adobe wall that we had found an oasis.

Inside, the ground floor opened into two rooms, one filled with a dozen or so tables, some chairs, clinking glasses, a bluish mist of cigarette smoke, the stench of cheap whiskey, and a dim neon glow across the faces of a few vacant-eyed men and women, most of whom stared silently at a hole in space somewhere behind their companions' heads. No animated chatter, no flirting barmaid hustling tips, and no loud jukebox rose above the even hum of a few overhead fans. I stood in a graveyard. This was where the dead evening went to be buried. Through a very wide opening, the smaller, darker room contained the shadowy outline of six or seven human forms of undetermined gender, three tables, and a raised platform, maybe a foot off the floor. The platform had two amplifiers, a drum set, an electric keyboard, a guitar laid across one amp, and a single microphone on a stand. The amplifiers were switched on, evident by the tiny pinpoints of red light, but the stage was uninhabited.

I gave a well-muscled doorman ten dollars. He nodded and directed us toward the larger room where we found an empty table set up with ice bucket and paper cups. Around us, a few people drank and chuckled. The atmosphere was radically different from the boisterous clubs we had visited earlier that evening – the ones where laughter hid the misery. Some patrons spoke to each other in whispers, and some mumbled into the air. No one paid much attention to a stocky, broad-shouldered kid with a shaved head and the slight girl tied to his arm and bouncing like a helium balloon into the misty room.

"Where's everyone getting their drinks?" I asked Summer.

"These places are BYOB," she said. "It's illegal to sell drinks after 2:00 a.m., and it's almost 3:00 a.m. now. You bring your own bottle of booze and the club gives you ice and sells mixers. They don't have these places in Indiana?"

"We have one place where I live called Lamey's Grove," I said. "It's a white concrete building in the middle of a field where people park their cars. A band called the Corvettes plays there every Saturday. No one drinks inside because off-duty cops work security and the crowd's mostly high school kids, so drinking is illegal. We'd all go out to our cars during breaks and sneak a few beers or a few shots of bourbon. If the cops caught you, they'd try to scare you and just confiscate your booze and take it home. I guess that was part of their deal--a little cash and all the alcohol they could steal."

"Are you afraid?" Summer asked.

"Of what?"

"Of going to war."

"I never really thought about it much. I was bored at home, so I joined the Marines."

"Don't you worry about what might happen?"

"You mean dying? Honestly, it never crossed my mind. I've always felt kind of magical, like the world is keeping something special in mind for me, and all I have to do is wait 'til it's my time to get it. Besides, they train us in the Marines to accept that death with honor is a part of life."

That youthful arrogance, enhanced by an illusion of immortality that was so much a part of my Midwestern, middle class, privileged upbringing during the early 1960's, drained away with my blood in a ditch by the side of Highway One near Hue just a few months later. It has been replaced by forty years of survivor's guilt and a slight limp. But before the fact is always more fun than after the fact. Rhetoric such as "death before dishonor" and "Semper Fidelis" is a believable part of some future reality until the actuality in present tense reveals there is no honor in getting blown to pieces by an artillery shell, and past tense proves no war deserves blind credulity.

Summer glared and looked dissatisfied with my answer but didn't respond. I needed alcohol. The Mexican beers and tequila from earlier in the evening had frayed the edges of my happy glow into a headache and trembling hands. Out of manly stupidity, I dismissed Summer's glare as an inability to understand manly things and left the table to beg. I found a soft-hearted fellow in a leather vest three tables away. He was willing to part with a half pint of Jim Beam for retail price plus a five dollar finder's fee, even though there were two more bottles stuck in his pockets, and he was sharing an open quart with three friends at his table.

Summer and I mixed the bourbon with ice and Coke-a-Cola. It tasted sweet, and in a few minutes I felt restored. In the smaller room, a short man with long hair had picked up the guitar and was tuning it. Then a thin man wearing glasses sat at the keyboard and pumped a few notes through one of the amps. The chaotic sounds mixed with feedback from a microphone center stage when the singer lifted it from the mike stand and turned his back to us. As he did, the drummer swirled the sticks across the snare drum and floor tom-tom while thumping the bass twice with his foot pedal. The building fell silent. Then the electric keyboard, followed by the squealing guitar, pierced the air as if a god had tied two lightning bolts together and they were fighting to unknot themselves.

I rode the sound into a world of dreams where thoughts shifted into flames and night bloomed into death and the wild scream of Vietnam swirled into my cup of Jim Beam. The voice rose like a banshee's cry above the music and became language. Suicidal and full of wonder. Omnipotent yet terrified. The color blue mixed with the scent of smoking wet wood. *You know that it would be untrue/you know that I would be a liar/if I were to say to you/girl we couldn't get much higher/come on baby light my fire.* Sweat seeped into my palms, and the ash of stars sifted over the crowd. I stumbled over the remnants of a generation's relinquished innocence and heard their small giggles. These ghosts of the future inside my head urged me to reach across the table and kiss the small girl who faced me, pretending that what we both needed had everything to do with the melody between us and not the loneliness of our lives.

Instead, I lit a cigarette, hoping the distraction of the acrid smoke in my lungs would allow the nonchalant look on my face to remain. Summer would be far more impressed by my indifference to the possibility that I was in the presence of Jim Morrison, Robby Kreiger, Ray Manzarek, and John Densmore than by the quivering jelly of my soul.

Yes, the Doors were sending me off to Vietnam. They were unannounced, and the stage was not well-lit. But the sound was unmistakable. When the song ended, I asked Summer in a trembling voice that could not be camouflaged if the band might actually be the real thing.

"It's impossible to tell without proper light. I've only seen them once. But, there's a good chance it is. A lot of popular bands stop by clubs in this area after their regular clubs close just to have some fun. I heard a group called Iron Butterfly a few blocks from here just last week. They bored me."

No one has ever verified that I had heard what I thought I heard and I never spoke with Summer again after that night. But, I did go to Vietnam the very next week and during the war I witnessed occurrences far more bizarre and dangerous than an impromptu concert by the Doors.

So, did I really see the mystical band by accident one evening in the late summer of 1967 or some good cover band similar in appearance? If I were a gambler like my father, I would say the odds were about equal to the chance of coming home from war alive. But I did survive. Was I meant to find some meaning above and beyond the incident itself? For a long time, I believed there had to be, but for a long time I believed also that America fought just wars.

Chapter Sixteen

Yesterday's News

"That old nag is as worthless as yesterday's news."

Old Man McCullogh, which was all I ever called him, used to repeat that statement to his "friends" each time one of us considered buying a horse whether we asked him for the advice, or not. Notice, I put quotes around the word friends because I'm not sure exactly what any of our relationships were in the cutthroat business of thoroughbred horse racing. We were all horse trainers who raced the Midwest circuit from Hawthorne Park through Churchill Downs and Ellis Park till we arrived in New Orleans at Fairgrounds in the winter and then started back north again every spring. Most of us competed for business, traveling in and out of each other's proximity and exchanging insults as a sign of masculine affection and respect. The insult part included James McCullogh, but never the business part.

The thing was, Old Man McCullogh with all his expertise and decades of experience never had a public racing stable. There was always some mystery surrounding the reason why not. Some said it had to do with his past criminal activity. Others believed the state racing stewards gave him a restricted license due to some horse doping incident from the ancient past. Once he got falling down drunk in the Ellis Park clubhouse and actually fell over on a crowd of bettors huddled around the bar. As he slid to the floor a .32 pistol squirted out of his back pocket and clattered across the concrete surface. Terrified, the crowd scattered. In reality, the most frightening aspect of that episode stemmed from the fact that he was able to stand and order another drink on his own. Nevertheless, the stewards suspended his license, the one that was already restricted, for the remainder of the meet. The security office held the gun till he left Ellis Park for the last time. The point being here that his trainer's license and reputation were never clear of one cloud or another long enough for him to develop a list of clients who would trust him with their expensive thoroughbreds.

I met him a few months before I began my own business. I was still working as stable foreman for Dan Wilson's twenty head of thoroughbreds. The job title spruced up the actual work, which was grooming horses and babysitting Dan's fiancé, Jade. Dan and McCullogh were drinking buddies and that meant they were together most waking hours of most days. The old man owned one horse at a time, usually crippled in some way, and when it finally broke down, McCullogh would send it to a farm and buy or claim another one, nursing it along for a few races until it earned his money back or became so badly injured it couldn't race either. The process cycled about every three or four months. He intended, always, that the newest horse would be the one that made him the "big score" leading to his retirement, which was his favorite delusion since for all practical purposes he was already retired.

When each horse failed to live up to his expectations, the runner became yesterday's news to him and he poured over the Daily Racing Form searching the past performances of hundreds of thoroughbreds for some hidden anomaly in a horse's racing history that only he was smart enough to correct and thus fulfill his dream. I never knew where the money to buy these horses came from, but it always appeared in his horseman's account at the racing secretary's office exactly when McCullogh needed it.

He wasn't nearly as old as he appeared, and he appeared ancient. His interior parts had either dried up or ulcerated from the constant influx of Budweiser and the ever-present pinch of Copenhagen snuff between his lower lip and gum. This gave his face the texture of gray parchment that had been wadded up and smoothed out unsuccessfully, and these habits killed him ultimately with stomach cancer. Being part Native American, he had no beard but had evidently shaved anyway as a younger man. Consequently, his cheeks and chin remained covered in thin patches of stubble sort of like a lawn that was partially seeded. He smiled frequently and exposed a mouthful of tobacco-stained teeth. His eyes twinkled till he got really drunk and then they became dead and more than a little scary.

I'd like to tell you that McCullogh had a keen sense of fashion, but I'm only a little bit of a liar. His black-rimmed bifocals were held together at every conceivable strategic place with masking tape. This was a result of having been broken against his face by someone else's fist repeatedly. He tended to get belligerent and mouthy when switching from Budweiser to Jim Beam before dark. Somewhere in his middle-age, the old horse trainer's hair had fallen out and he covered the baldness with a felt cap with the earflaps down even when the thermometer read 100 degrees. On most days, McCullogh wore a long sleeved shirt that had been white at some point and alternating brown or black polyester pants held aloft by both belt and suspenders. This ensemble was completed with suede Hush Puppy shoes spotted with tobacco stained spittle.

One Saturday in September – the year was 1977, I believe. I had won a race at a track in northern Kentucky that was then called Latonia. I spied Old Man McCullogh in his favorite lawn chair leaning against his stall wall when I brought my horse back from the testing barn after the race. He looked forlorn, more than usual, and I asked him what had happened.

"That old horse of mine chipped his knee breezing this morning."

"That knee was chipped when you claimed him."

"Yeah, but I felt a new piece of bone floating around the joint."

The injury was a common one, especially among cheaper bred horses because their leg conformations were never perfect. Without being almost perfect, the pressure exerted by one skinny leg at a time pegging into the hard track surface at forty miles an hour by a thousand pounds of body weight always ended up chipping or cracking or pulling something.

"What's the plan?"

"Dope him up and drop him down in class. If somebody claims him, then I can start over. He's yesterday's news, buddy boy."

The moral and ethical questions that might have arisen such as the safety of running an injured horse and the prospect of selling that horse to an unsuspecting buyer never entered the old man's mind. It probably wouldn't have bothered me much either in the same situation. In this way we were very much like today's corporate CEO's, only without all the money. Before you render judgment on this practice, please remember that a drowning man will latch onto anything available to stay afloat and on the bush league racing circuit, we were all drowning men.

I asked McCullogh if I could buy his dinner since my pockets were flush from winning the previous race. Never one to turn down a free drink or meal, he agreed, and we drove in his pickup truck to an overpriced steak house with gaudy red and blue carpet and black lighting that made it almost impossible to see the food. This turned out to be a positive thing. There's a reason I'm including this anecdote. By the time the story is finished, you will understand a little more about how complicated humans are. Just when you think you've got one pegged one way or another, they end up showing you that everyone has a positive and negative tug of war inside them all the time and sometimes, it's difficult to tell which one is going to win.

I ordered a T-bone steak and he ordered a ground round steak.

"You understand that's hamburger, right?" I said.

"What the fuck are you talking about? You think I can't read? It says right here on the menu – steak."

He had begun to slur his words badly, a sure sign that the beer had been put away and the whiskey bottle opened. When the waitress brought our meals, his turned out to be hamburger and he screamed at the top of lungs. "Hey, this ain't a fucking steak. It's a hamburger."

"It's what you asked for," I said, as the waitress ran back to the table.

I calmed her down with a ten dollar bill and convinced Old Man McCullogh to eat. He did. Right after he pulled a huge wad of Copenhagen snuff from under his lip and threw it on the carpet, he picked the meat up with his hands and gnawed it away as the grease and snuff dripped from his chin. My appetite ruined, I made him drive me back to my barn. I had no idea where he went, but an hour later the security guard came over to get me saying I had a phone call at the back gate. It was McCullogh exercising his phone call privilege from the Florence, Kentucky, jail. I bailed him out with the last of the money I won at the races and swore we were done. With all his horse knowledge and all I could still learn, the incorrigible old bastard was more trouble than he would ever be worth. Then, we shipped to Churchill Downs to get ready for the fall race meet.

There was a hot walker there that everyone called Rip. Who knew what his real name had been. Rip worked for a big fat slob of a trainer named Harold Foyle and got paid at the end of each day just enough money to buy two or three pints of Mad Dog 20/20 or Gallo port wine, whichever was on sale. There was little difference between those fine wines and wood alcohol or Sterno. Drink this stuff for very long and you might as well have been drinking ground glass. I have no idea what was in either brand only that Rip went on a bender for two weeks about a month after we arrived in Louisville, ending up blind in a pool of his own puked up and pissed out blood. Old Man McCullogh found him behind the spit – drug testing – barn one night lying on a bed of gravel and helped him get up. Then, he drove him to Foyle's barn. The guy was barely conscious and his breathing very shallow, at least according to what I was told later. Harold Foyle fired him on the spot and told McCullogh to get him out of the barn.

I found out the next day that the old man rode in the ambulance with Rip, sat with him in the ER, and paid the bill. He got him checked into rehab at the Jefferson County Home for the Indigent, and signed the papers to pay any extra costs. He visited Rip every day for two weeks. When Rip had dried out enough, McCullogh brought him back to the track and let him bunk in his tack room till someone hired him. I have no idea what motivated the old man to care for Rip in such a manner. I don't believe it was guilt altogether. He was too arrogant in many ways to feel much guilt or seek repentance for his past actions. When I thought it might be kindness and asked him, he laughed in my face and said, "Don't bring that sentimental horse shit up to me. Whatever I done for Rip is yesterday's news and none of your business." Regardless of his reasoning, Jim McCullogh solidified one of my father's proverbs for me. *No matter how thin you slice bread, it always has two sides.* A human can be a real prick but maintain the capacity for good and a good hearted soul is capable of great evil. Never judge a person as absolutely one way or another because you sell the human race short when you do.

Chapter Seventeen

How It All Connects

Henry Fielding once said, "All nature wears one universal grin." What Fielding didn't say was whether the grin happened to be pleasant or sardonic. Most of the time, it's a little of both. Sanden King, one of the three horses my father bought initially as yearlings in 1975, had become a workhorse in my racing stable. He paid his way by placing consistently and winning a race on occasion. I had entered him in the fourth race on an Ellis Park program one day in the summer of 1979. The horse carried two small bone chips in his fetlock, or ankle. By standing his front legs in ice water up to the knees an hour before a race, I pulled the inflammation out temporarily. The horse liked it, remaining motionless with his sleepy head hanging over the stall webbing. So did Barrel.

Yes, the same huge, bulbous-eyed, diabetic drunk that worked in Dan Wilson's stable alongside his buddies Wally, Hector, and Octavio when I did now worked for me. Worked is the wrong verb. The fat man's health had deteriorated so much over the short time I had known him that he was barely able to hobble around the barn with a bottle of beer and not lose his breath. Dan fired him at the Churchill Downs meet in June of that year and it must have been like losing one of the family. He fell out of favor with his boss by passing out drunk before feeding the entire stable full of hungry race horses one night. Two of the horses injured themselves by kicking the stall walls in anger before the morning work crew arrived. Much the same as a Christian who sins against the Holy Spirit, Barrel had committed the only unpardonable act in the Hard Boot bible. He put his own desire for alcohol above the safety of his charges.

I had spent one night in a fleabag motel off Highway 41 in Evansville, Indiana, when I shipped my horses into Ellis Park in July for the beginning of the meet and happened to see the guy struggling to enter a room a few doors down from mine. That's how I learned the story of his demise at Churchill the month before. He took me into his filthy home, the floor littered with candy bar wrappers and empty beer cans. That sickly, sweet, acetone stench of alcoholic ketoacidosis was soaked into the air to such an extent that bile rose in my throat. It was all I could do to hold down my lunch. Barrel explained that Dan had given him a few dollars to get by for a while. The old boy hitched a ride on a horse van and came to Ellis in search of work. He had spent the past week in this room, coming out only to stumble across the plaza for booze and junk food. Now, his money had evaporated and another day's rent had come due. Never comfortable enough in my self-importance to resist a sob story, I paid his rent and drove him to the barn with me the next morning where I set up an old army cot in the tack room and let him hang around while we went about our regular routine with the horses. I bought him food each day and watched him eat it. Although I knew better, I supplied him with a ration of beer because he refused to go to the hospital. There was no contingency on the track for dealing with delirium tremens.

Barrel formed an immediate bond with Sanden King, which takes me back to Henry Fielding's quote regarding Nature's sense of humor and the incomprehensible nature of those universal connections that are occasionally made between beasts of differing species. The King had become a weaver, meaning the twenty-three hours a day the gelding was forced to spend in a twelve foot by twelve foot stall made him a nervous wreck. He stood at the entrance of his stall with his head thrust into the walking area commonly called "the shed row." Dancing back and forth from right front leg to left front leg, he would throw his massive head to and fro as if it were a huge equine metronome. Besides being annoying, the habit eventually proved debilitating. Sanden King lost weight, his ankles began to show signs of inflammation from the stress, and his racing ability slackened. I bought a Nubian goat and put it in the stall with him. They became playmates immediately, but rather than replace bad habits with constructive ones, the goat soon began weaving with the horse.

Almost the instant Barrel entered the barn, he remembered Sanden King and vice-versa. The ritual of standing the horse in a tub of ice to keep fluid from building in his ankles became a daily one.

Old Barrel always sat holding a leather lead shank attached to Sanden King's halter. They seemed to pacify each other, sometimes snoring in unison. On this particular racing day, I left them together and went to the track kitchen, grabbing sandwiches and coffee for us. My plan was to return and ready the gelding for his race with brush, curry comb, and hoof pick. As usual then, I would wait until a few minutes before our race, put the bridle on Sanden King, and give him to the pony boy. The rider and pony would lead the horse to the paddock in the grandstand area for saddling while Barrel and I drove around and met them. The big guy could no longer cover the half mile on foot.

As the cook bagged up my food, the track kitchen's screen door flew open and Wally, who still worked for Dan Wilson in another barn and hung around with Barrel every afternoon, came rushing to the counter.

"Hurry up, hurry up. Oh God, you gotta hurry the fuck up."

His trembling hand shook me hard. Instinctively raising my hands to protect my face, I stared into his frightened eyes and focused, trying to remember where we were and who screamed in my ear. The old groom looked horrified. Even his usual gray pallor was bleached white.

"What the hell's the matter with you?"

"Barrel won't wake up."

"He'd better be getting King ready for the race."

"No, you don't understand. He won't wake up."

The tremor in the man's voice made me nervous. Reaching out, I laid my hand on Wally's shoulder. "Slow down. You're not making any sense."

"I'm telling you, I can't make him open his eyes. He's just sitting there next to Sanden King and he feels cold."

Hustling back to the barn with Wally lagging behind, I assessed what may have been a hostile scene quickly like I learned to do in Vietnam. Initially, everything looked the way it should have looked. The horses all napped in the afternoon swelter. Fans hummed and horse tails rustled as flies were swatted. Nothing else broke the silence. Sanden King's head flopped over the webbing as he stood in his ice bucket and rested his nose on Barrel's shoulder. The big man seemed to have become a gargoyle, a silent sentry sitting quietly, eyes closed, hands folded around a beer can in his lap. On the track, the John Deere tractor pulled the starting gate down into the mile chute, preparing for the next race. Some horses and grooms began to walk by on their way back to the barns, all soaked with after race sweat. Some walked by on their way to the grandstand paddock area for a new race. A loony cat perched on the concrete ledge in front of the stall and licked its front paws as if it had just finished a large meal. Flies swarmed over the steaming muck pit. Everything looked so normal and peaceful that I knew it wasn't.

I couldn't really put my finger on what was wrong, but the small hairs on the back of my neck stood straight up. Adrenaline surged through my arms and legs. I felt my pulse quicken. If this had been the jungle, I would have expected gunfire any second. But there was no jungle. No, only the slightly tilted roof of a one story wood and concrete horse barn and this barn stood with a long line of other barns on earth that belonged to some rich family in the state of Kentucky and the state of Kentucky belonged to the union of states that made up the United States. No. This wasn't the jungle, but the smell of urine and clover hay filled my nose and I realized that no matter where I stood nothing was safe from the decay of living and the rot of time.

Moving past the water tap and the coiled hose and down the center of the shed row, I reached Barrel quickly with Wally shuffling behind me. No blood throbbed through the carotid artery. No breath rattled the cellophane off of a cigarette pack as I held a piece under the nose. Sanden King lifted his head quizzically, nuzzled his buddy, and stared at the horses on the track warming up for the next race. The front of Barrel's tent-sized jeans were soaked with piss where the man had voided himself.

"He's gone ain't he," said Wally as if the word dead might make the absence of life contagious. I stepped into the stall and lifted the horse's legs from the ice. There was nothing to be done for the corpse and King should have been taken out of the ice. The next race called would be ours. I was all business now. Emotion was weakness and weakness could be fatal. The numbness that had overcome me in the war and that I wanted to cleanse from my psyche returned instantly as if it were a child playing hide seek, just out of reach but close enough to reassert its presence with very little effort.

"Get the grooming box and get this horse cleaned up. I've got to hang his bridle on him and go to the paddock as soon as this next race is over."

"I can't."

"Damnit Wally. Don't be stupid. Your buddy's dead, probably his heart. *Move.*"

"I can't look at him." He shook violently, sweat spinning from him as if he were a wet dog. I thought the old man was going to faint and if that happened he would block the stall door. It irritated me when I had to deal with fear, and yet I felt sorry for Barrel at the same time. No, I won't say I felt sorry. I'll say I wanted to feel sorry because I *thought* that's what I should feel. This is one of the problems with Post Traumatic Stress Disorder, something undiagnosed and unnamed at this time in America that affected tens of thousands of Vietnam veterans. You know you're supposed to feel something because you're human and so you consciously conjure up something akin to an emotion, but it's usually the wrong emotion and hyperbolic.

"Sit down on that bale of straw and put your head back."

"There's nothing I could've done," said Wally.

"I know that."

"What if I could've done something?"

"He died. People die all the time. It was always out of your hands."

"He just disappeared. He was here and now he isn't."

"He went nowhere. He's right in front of us, at least his body is. You didn't stop his heart, did you?"

"No."

"Then, like I said, this doesn't have anything to do with you or me."

I slid under the stall webbing, raising my hand to the dead man's lukewarm cheek. He must have been dead no longer than a few minutes. Wally said the body was cold, but obviously he had been too frightened to touch the skin. The book of Revelation, chapter 3 and verse sixteen flashed into my mind, although looking back on it now I have no idea where it came from because I knew nothing of the Bible. *So because thou art lukewarm, and neither hot nor cold, I will spew thee out of my mouth.* Barrel had been spewed from some god's mouth. Not much of a revelation. Everybody gets spewed sooner or later. I looked over at Wally.

"Got your wind back old man?"

"Yeah."

"Then go to the guard shack and have security send the track ambulance to the barn. I'll get Sanden King ready."

Picking up a currycomb, I began swirling motions on the horse's coat. As soon as the comb hit him, the gelding knew it was race time, bucking in the stall and nipping playfully at my arms. This was what he lived for, to run and compete, a simple life for which he was well-fed and treated like an imprisoned demigod.

"Settle down big boy. Save that energy for the race. I want you to make some money today." I worked the comb quickly, then a stiff brush through the mane and tail, then a soft brush over the horse's face, shoulders, withers, and rump, then a cloth rag polishing the sleek coat like it was the finish on a Mercedes. Finally, I lifted each leg, running the hoof pick over the soles of the hooves to clean away any dirt or manure. All the time I worked, Barrel perched against the barn wall protecting his trust from some distant place now. I talked to the body like the corpsmen used to do in the morgue at Danang.

"Just like old times for me, Hard Boot. I seem to work better with dead bodies lying around. How about that? Pretty sick, huh. Well, I always said my training in 'Nam would come in handy. I'd like to feel something for you right now, but nothing I felt would help you and it certainly wouldn't make me handle this horse better. Nope, you're dead and I'm alive. That's good for me and bad for you."

As soon as the words left my mouth, I felt like crying, but didn't. The tears didn't stream, they just sort of swelled in the corners of my eyes and held on. Why the hell would I cry anyway? I'd seen better men die. This man meant nothing to me, an old drunk with a bad heart that finally quit. Hearts do that all the time. Sometimes they don't quit, sometimes something stops them like a piece of lead or the loss of blood before they wear out. Red spots danced across the straw. I squinted. They disappeared, replaced by a sort of white blindness. The whole barn became a vacuum, void of sound. The fans stopped humming, the wind quit strumming the hay, the low wail of the radio disappeared. Then I heard a thump in the distance and another and another. Soon the thump became a steady pounding behind my eardrums. All the different sounds had been swallowed by the silence of Barrel's heart and emerged as the single sound of my own. I opened my eyes and looked at the carcass.

"You motherfucker, leave me alone."

Terrified suddenly by my own mortality, I ducked under the stall webbing and jumped into the middle of the shed row. Out of breath, I sucked at the hot, humid air and held it inside momentarily letting it burn my lungs to insure myself I was still alive. I opened a bottle of isopropyl alcohol to rub King down and keep the horse cool, like my mother used to do when I had a high fever as a child. The unmistakable scent of the colorless liquid made me lightheaded at first, and then it transported me back in time. I didn't understand it at the time, but looking back I can see myself entering one of those intrusive thoughts that infected my brain periodically the first decade away from combat.

Everything was white. I was in a room, a place the Marine Corps made me go before I could move around with crutches. My shrapnel wounds were healing, but I was still in traction from a broken leg. The room was frigid and fluorescent white. Eric Clapton's high-pitched guitar played in my head. The strings wound around Jack Bruce's words - *I'll wait in this place where the sun never shines - I'll wait in this place where the shadows run from themselves - In the white room with black curtains at the station.* I understood the sterility of the song. If not for the olive drab jungle fatigues on the doctors, I would have sworn a mistake had been made. This was the snowy white South Pole, not sweaty Southeast Asia. It wasn't just the absence of color or the monotony of artificial light. The constant hum of the air conditioner and the dripping of a faulty faucet into a huge stainless steel sink entranced me. Every movement of my arms and legs seemed to be made by someone outside my body. The scent of rubbing alcohol clawed its way into my nose and nested there till everything smelled like isopropyl. It was the hospital at Cam Rahn Bay. In a war zone, hospitals are for the dead and dying, the battered and broken, the ripped and sliced, a warehouse for the permanently damaged who wait to be shipped somewhere else and hidden away. The alcohol clung to everything in the ward and ever since then when the stench caught me off guard it took me back there. It opened old wounds new.

Was I completely fucking nuts? It was a thought that occupied a lot of my time since the war. But here came that recurring life preserving phrase that if you thought you were crazy, you had to be sane or else you wouldn't have thought you were crazy in the first place. So, slowly I recapped the alcohol bottle. As I lifted my head toward the sun and closed my eyes again, the jumping in my mind stopped. The normal sounds of life returned.

"Hey buddy, what the hell are you doing?" An ambulance was stopped before me. "Are you okay? You were dancing around like a crazy man," said one of the paramedics.

"A wasp. I got a wasp under my shirt."

"Let me help you."

"It's gone now. The body's over here. Where's Wally?"

"He's gone to the grandstand to find Dan Wilson. What happened?"

"As near as I can tell, the old man had a heart attack or something while he was sitting here watching the horse."

"Is that Sanden King?"

"Yeah. It is."

"The hell you say. Think he'll win today? I'd like to bet on him. I've won some cash on him before."

"He's got a real good shot, but you know racing. You've got to always expect the unexpected. Hell, if I knew for sure what was going to happen, I'd be a wealthy man."

The second paramedic climbed from the cab of the ambulance, opened the rear doors and pulled a folded stretcher out onto the road. The bell rang from the starting gate at the end of the mile chute. The race before ours began. By the time the race ended, the corpse had been loaded like a sack of grain onto the ambulance with the help of five stable curious onlookers. It was called dead weight for a reason.

Two security guards and a small crowd, drawn by the appearance of the ambulance, gathered in front of the barn. One of the grooms from another barn offered to help with the horse. I put the racing bridle on King, made sure the bit was set right in the mouth, and tied a simple slipknot in the reins to keep them from dangling. For the first time in a long time the idea that I didn't have to control each circumstance in my life, no, the idea that I *couldn't* control it became strangely comforting. It freed me from being responsible for randomness.

The groom pulled my horse from the stall and handed him over to my pony boy, who hooked his leather lead through the D-ring on the bridle. At first, Sanden King walked beside the pony quietly. Did this animal know his friend had died in his presence? I wasn't sure of the answer, but horse and man certainly seemed to have had a kinship that went beyond horse and stable hand. By the time we walked onto the main track and toward the grandstand area, King had raised his head. His ears pricked at the sound of other horses being led past him. He started to prance, a little at first, but within a few hundred yards he looked like a horse floating on air and became almost impossible to handle.

Chapter Eighteen

Back Home Again

Many intelligent people scoff at the idea that man and beast have a spiritual connection and I confess my ignorance of such things, as well. But, I do know and it is a matter of record that, after the ambulance carted Barrel away, I led Sanden King to the paddock, saddled him and watched him run the best race of his career, winning by almost a full furlong. I believe it was his way of telling the old man goodbye.

Following a death, people feel obligated to say things like "life goes on" or "the sun will still come up tomorrow" or "he's in a better place." None of that describes in accurate terms the idea that death exposes the raw truth that we are all disposable and will, ultimately, be disposed of by a tumor, a bullet, a drunk driver, a broken heart, or some random occurrence never before imagined and when it happens, the people still breathing will continue with the process of this process between womb and grave we call life. It is true that memory and presence are linked inexorably and in infinite ways. But, how much time the dead spend as shadows defined only as vague memories or paralyzing specters in our conscious depends entirely on what wrenches us back to the present tense and how fast.

In my case I had a business to run that dominated my waking moments. I met a young woman who became my wife. Horses came and went. Races got won and lost. Each day provided a new series of immediate circumstances that required attention. Time for reflection on death became so scarce that I almost forgot it existed. It wasn't like the old fat man had been a close friend, or that his self-destructive alcoholism appeared as a rare occurrence on the race track. At Oaklawn Park in Hot Springs, Arkansas, I once saw a security guard fire an imaginary .45 pistol at a group of flying pink monkeys that tormented a grizzled old hot walker in order to calm his delirium tremens caused by the three-day absence of Thunderbird wine. The monkeys disappeared. A year later in Hot Springs once again, I hired a man known only as "Doc" around the racing circuit. I paid this stable hand a few dollars every day and every day he walked out the back gate of the track, crossed the street, and bought a bottle of Seagram's 7 Whiskey. Then he promptly returned to the tack room where he laid on an old army cot and drank that bottle. Each morning, I shook him awake and he stumbled around the barn cooling out the horses after their morning exercise.

One day about halfway through the race meet, I came in at 6a.m. and found Doc lying on the cot unconscious and soaked in his own piss.

"Doc, wake up," I yelled and banged a feed tin on the concrete wall. The stench of urine and vomit gagged me, but by concentrating on the perfume of molasses and leather that hung around the edges of the disgusting odor I managed to avoid throwing up myself. "Come on, Doc. You should have had the horses fed already. The rest of the crew will be here in a few minutes. We've got horses to train."

The guy struggled to push himself into a sitting position. Each hair on his head that wasn't tangled into a ball shot off in different directions giving me the impression that he had stuck a finger in a light socket and electrified his body. His jaundiced cheeks were shadowed by gray stubble and his eyes glazed over like ceramic blue ashtrays. Doc lit a cigarette and coughed out the first puff.

"Jesus. I pissed myself."

"No kidding. Have you got any other clothes in here?"

He pointed with a long slender finger toward an army duffel bag standing at attention in the corner of the room beneath a row of leather bridles that hung from a wooden shelf. I upturned the bag quickly. Three suits labeled *Botany 500* spilled across the concrete floor. The expensive brown and gray material lay in a wrinkled and dusty pile, but the bag was not empty. I shook it again. Two pieces of rolled parchment fell onto the suits. Unrolling one, I stared at the writing wanting to believe it was a forgery of some kind and yet knowing deep down it really wasn't. In my hands I held a diploma from Harvard Law School. I set it gently on a barrel of rolled oats and picked up the other one, an MBA from the same Ivy League school.

"Doc?"

"Yeah, I know. I had a good job once. I had my own law firm in Boston."

"What the fuck are you doing drunk in Arkansas."

"I was keeping some creative financial records for some guys." At this point, he pushed his nose to the side. "Guido's who weren't real nice. The feds popped me, the state disbarred me, and my wife left for someone who still had an income. End of a sad fucking story."

"Jesus, Doc, you could be doing a lot better than this." I swirled my right hand around the musty and dank concrete block room in an expansive gesture.

"I could also be at the bottom of a river with cement overshoes. I got some unsavory characters who still want to talk to me about where their money went when the feds caught me. I mean, come on, I didn't want to do any jail time. I sang like a fucking bird. There's no better place to disappear than the track, unless it might be a carnival."

There's really no way to ascertain what happened to Doc. He was an intelligent and articulate man in the throes of horrible demons of his own making. Once I left the south end of my racing circuit, which consisted of a few weeks in New Orleans and a few weeks in Hot Springs, my wife and I returned to the Midwest. Being a reasonable man, I can assume that, given his chronic drinking habits, Doc went the way of old Barrel, but I don't have any idea really. One thing I know for sure, as smart as he was Doc was way off base about the best way to disappear. Hiding on the track or the carnival had some benefits in that department. But, you still couldn't disappear from yourself. Ultimately, that's the only way to vanish, to give up self-centered desires, to make propitiatory sacrifices by eliminating your most enjoyable flaws, and trading your old life for something brand new that is greater than the sum of its apparent parts. I came to this realization when my first child was born in 1980, a beautiful girl.

***

There was always the snow in the winter of 1980 and the frozen track where the horses bruised the soles of their feet or burned the backs of their fetlocks. I had never ventured further north with my horses than my home in the southwestern tip of Indiana, thirty miles away from Ellis Park, a racetrack just across the Kentucky border. But, I came north this particular year because the old-time horsemen, the ones whose only home had ever been the tracks on the Midwestern bush league racing circuit, said the pickings were easier at Hawthorne and Sportsman's. No one with really good horses that could win purse money in Florida, Louisiana, or Arkansas would be dumb enough to race in sub-zero weather. "Go take the cash from the fools, kid," they said. Because I had a new daughter and wanted more security for the first time in my life, a sanctuary from the evils of the world that I believed only money could provide, I heeded their advice.

The thoroughbreds in my public stable were good ones for the most part, solid and consistent runners as long as I kept them in the class where they belonged, and true to form they ran well at Hawthorne. However, I was a new trainer to this part of the racing circuit and, as such, didn't exercise much political clout or have any important financial connections. Trainers with either one of those received good stabling areas near the main track. Trainers with both got treated like royalty. The racing secretary did assign me my own special barn across the road at Sportsman's. That track was closed during the Hawthorne meet in November the way Hawthorne would be closed in December for the Sportsman's meet. Consequently, when one side filled on a preferential basis, the other side got the overflow. That particular year I happened to be the only overflow and as such had an entire racetrack to myself. I assumed, given the magnanimity of the racing secretary, I would get my own barn once again in December but on the Hawthorne side.

Resignation was an important aspect of life in racing. I resigned myself to walking my horses across a busy asphalt road in subzero weather through a long tunnel to the paddock and after each race we ran, walking them back again. The horses didn't mind the cold nearly as much as I did.

I arrived in Cicero, Illinois, with my extended family, which included my wife, my three month old daughter, one of my wife's sisters who worked as a groom, a hot walker running away from his juvenile detention in Kentucky, and an exercise rider with aspirations of becoming the first female Willie Shoemaker. We lived in three separate dorm rooms above the stalls in our barn. The rooms were small and warm with tiled floors and concrete walls painted a rotted peach color, and once you got used to the constant smell of wet straw, horse liniment, and manure, quite comfortable. We slept on mattresses laid across the floor. Our furniture consisted of a used baby bed and a black and white TV set with a clothes hanger for an antenna.

To a more civilized American, this may have seemed an impossible living arrangement, but I had become a Hard Boot, a special breed of racetracker willing to sacrifice the American Dream of split-level homes, picket fences, and 2.5 children that my generation was sold by the Eisenhower era for the adrenaline rush produced by hoof beats thundering down the last stretch of sand and clay toward an invisible finish line and the winner's circle beyond it. My wife had come from a huge family that spent their entire lives in one aspect or another of the horse business. Basically, I became a Hard Boot-in-law.

I liked Cicero. Once you got past the fact that it was a ghetto suburb of Chicago and had its own coterie of mentally deficient criminals, the city had much to recommend it. Cicero was a tangible, cement manifestation of the yin and yang of life. For example, the first night there we parked our cars in the well-lit, well-guarded security lot between the two race tracks and walked up the block to a small wooden building on a nearby corner. It looked like all the other frame houses surrounding it, but was, in fact, Sporty Joe's Steak House, home of the biggest T-bones in the Midwest. This fact did not surprise me as I had read Sinclair Lewis' famous turn of the century novel called *The Jungle*, an expose of the gargantuan meat packing industry that powered Chicago's economy. The dining room was balmy, a wonderful respite from the icy "Hawk" bearing down on us from Lake Michigan, and clouded with the scent of A-1 sauce, spicy fries, garlic, and grilled beef. The waitresses were friendly, the drunks happy, and the meal delicious. I ate a twenty ounce medium rare porterhouse that was so tender it sliced with my butter knife.

While we ruminated and meditated and drank brandy with our coffee, a person or persons unknown removed the T-tops from an exercise rider's Camaro Z-28. In the same secure parking lot, a genius with a criminal mind that must have rivaled Lex Luther's broke the windshield out of my sister-in-law's car so as to steal her two-dollar Saint Christopher medal hanging from the rearview mirror. He must not have been able to tell that the doors were unlocked in the shadows of the huge security lamp. As everyone surveyed the damage on a full stomach, I walked to the guard shack and asked the rather pleasant and plump man hunched over an electric heater if he'd seen anything out of the ordinary.

"No," he said, "just the usual run-of-the-mill vandals and thieves."

"Do you ever try and stop them?"

"Oh, hell no. Too dangerous."

"Do you ever call the police?"

"Phone's broke."

We retired to our rooms and considered the impracticality of driving a Z-28 without T-tops in the Lake Michigan winter. The next night this exercise rider, a friend of mine from Arkansas, left the keys in the ignition and, sure enough, the car was missing within a few hours. He called the insurance company and had the whole thing replaced much quicker than if he would've had to wait on new tops shipped from the factory.

I made a lot of money that winter, just like the old-timers said I would, but by late January the horses were getting sore from running over frozen track surfaces. Hay prices in Chicago soared to nine dollars a bale, which in 1980/81 was a fortune. The people around me developed a surly winter depression, and in the twenty-by-twenty dorm room, a virulent strain of cabin fever incubated.

My daughter, now five months old, cried most nights with colic, or maybe she just vocalized a reflection of my own growing anxiety. Whatever was going on with her awakened in me memories of my own childhood. It hadn't been like this at all. I had an apple tree right outside my bedroom window, a huge backyard full of mystical promise, my own dog, a tricycle with red streamers dangling from the handlebars, a mother who baked pecan pies frequently, and a father who had time to play catch every evening after he came home tired from work. Thinking about all these things I couldn't help but remember where I'd enjoyed them as a child.

If you had grown up as I did surrounded by corn and

soybean fields, unencumbered by the labyrinth of streets and congested traffic common to urban life, then you would understand my acute claustrophobia. If you had ever slept with the doors of your house unlocked, ate fresh vegetables and unprocessed homemade ice cream, played baseball from the time you could crawl, and believed once in Santa Claus, then you might sense how easily my memories developed a romantic impetus of their own. The misery of wintertime in Cicero began to outweigh its financial benefits. My daughter deserved better. My daughter deserved to grow up in a "special" place.

So I found another trainer for my father's horses and sold my equipment. It wasn't difficult, and it didn't take long. The horses were worthy, and I had always kept the saddles, bridles, and grooming gear in good shape. By the time the top layer of ice began to melt, I turned our old station wagon south and headed for the southern tip of Indiana. I received no argument from John Bill. According to his value system, no grandchild of his should have been raised like a gypsy anyway. The trainer who took over the horses was known and respected by my father and my "luck" had been good enough for so long, I'm sure he expected it to run out soon anyway. I always had the feeling that Dad saw my endeavors in any enterprise as subject to the whim of some external fate, good or bad, because he saw me as slightly broken, incapable of making things work on my own – especially any effort related to economics. And, he was right. I have the business sense of a rock, which is why I'm a writer I guess.

I can't say that I felt no regret. I loved working with horses, the freedom of being my own boss, the excitement of competition at a professional level, and a wad of money bulging in my pocket after a good race meet. However, something greater than these sensory rewards and pleasures pulled at me. I had an overwhelming desire to give my daughter a real childhood like the one I'd had. That desire required certain abstract, yet basic, things – stability security, joy, and love. All of these concepts could only be joined together and secured by a singular sense of place and time. For me, the world traveler, the gypsy, the vagabond, The Don Quixote in dungarees, any sense of place was centered in my memory of southern Indiana – home. Any sense of a truly joyful time for me remained barely memorable and embellished by my imagination as that pre-pubescent period before my innocence was shattered by the Vietnam War. For as much as I fought with my father over our differences in ideology, the actuality of my upbringing was fairly common for the time, even privileged. I didn't realize it then, but the fact that my father loved me and I loved him generated the need to argue. He wanted me to be my own man, to exercise my own will as long as it coincided with his. By providing tangible security and stability, he provided the freedom for us to dispute those distinctions. Is this normal? I have no idea. Did it work? It worked, except when it didn't. Am I equivocating here? Yes, I'm human.

Chapter Nineteen

Temporary Sanctuary

When I drove out the back gate of Hawthorne Race Track, it was to come home. I was forced by lack of skills to change jobs several times. I was blessed with a son in 1982 who, like my daughter, is now fully grown and also a very good person, much less flawed of character than his father. That's the best any parent can hope for, and probably what my dad hoped for me and where I fell short of the goal.

My parents and several friends have died along the way. Most of the retail shops that once surrounded the county courthouse closed their doors years ago, replaced by video arcades, fast-food restaurants, and a Super Wal-Mart on the west side of town, a phenomena common to rural America. My daughter and son got to know their grandparents, play Frisbee in Lafayette Park, own a puppy, join various youth groups, pick mushrooms, fish, and live in a real house rather than a stable. These proved to be positive things for both of them.

I'd like to say the move became a positive thing for me as well. But, in a few years I ended up restless and sour again, unable to maintain a relationship with my wife. We were soon divorced, my third. She returned to the only life we had known together on the racetrack and I spent several years raising my two children alone. The next decade became a period of intense reflection for me and period of regression for America. I discovered a thing called post-traumatic stress disorder had damaged my life and the country discovered Ronald Reagan. With some healing, I managed to marry again and, if longevity is a marker, this fourth one appears to be working. All of these details may show up someday in another story, along with my descent into religion and my resurrection through books. I'm thinking about writing that one even now. In the meantime, I'm going to follow Flannery O'Connor's advice and quit telling this one story because this one story has reached the end of its dramatic action. Don't get me wrong, I consider myself a picaresque hero of modernity not unlike <u>Don Quixote</u>. Consequently, you've been privy to an episode only.

Epilogue

When Churchill Downs Corporation from Louisville bought Ellis Park, they removed the whole thing, lock, stock, and barrel from its metaphorical Indiana roots. By that I mean most of the boundary between Indiana and Kentucky is recognized as the mid-point of the Ohio River. However, for over a century, the two states have argued about a small patch of land along Highway 41 on the Indiana, or northern, side of the river. Since the ground on which the race track was built in 1922 lay north of the water and since pari-mutuel wagering on horse races violated a prohibition in the Indiana Constitution until the late 1990's, the track could have never opened without a court decision that stipulated the Ohio River deviated from its original course in the 19th century. An act of God had left this postage stamp of land belonging to Kentucky dry enough for legalized horse racing and gambling while surrounded on all other sides by the sovereign state of Indiana. It was a miracle of Mosaic proportions brought on by the prayers of faithful punters and articulate lawyers. Indiana investors put money into the track. Horse families from Evansville and points north worked and raced there. For several decades Ellis Park was the only real horse track that Hoosiers could lay any claim to and lose their hard earned wages at.

Like an arthritic old race horse feels the rain coming, I feel the change in atmosphere already when I enter the new office of the Racing Secretary. The fresh paint smell clings to my nose and the prim, proper, high decibel greeting of an overly-anxious assistant grates in my ears. The décor is efficient and metallic. Each administrator and accountant works at separate cubicles. The coffee pot brews flavored gourmet coffee. *No Smoking* signs plaster the walls. I remember the days when this office was located in a cavernous barn-like structure just off the grandstand area. The old

Hard Boots lounged around the doorway, spitting tobacco juice onto the gravel outside, chomping on cigars, arguing about what horse could carry what weight and which jockey had the best hands. Mostly, I remember my father, a man I idolized as a child, hated as a teenager, and grew to respect when we joined forces in the business of racing horses.

***

Bob Jackson is a thin man in his mid-fifties. He has a firm handshake and a smile that says life is pretty much okay. His current position as Director of Racing proves just how hard it is to put the racetrack out of your mind and heart once it worms its way in.

Bob's father trained thoroughbreds at Ellis Park when old man Ellis was still growing soybeans in the infield to earn extra cash. By the time he was eleven in 1953, Bob was sneaking under the back fence and galloping horses with the jockeys in the gray dawn. He became a pretty fair rider in the 1960's, but a bad spill and subsequent injury cut short his career. Bob left the track and started a construction business. Even though that business was successful, when Ruth Adkins gave him an opportunity 15 years later to work in the Racing Secretary's office, he walked away from hammers, nails, and concrete and never looked back.

"If it wasn't for Ruth, I'd probably be building houses still."

I met Ruth, the woman who ran this track for the Ellis's for three decades when I was a green kid in 1978. My upgrade from groom to trainer was so recent that the Polaroid snapshot on the license hadn't fully developed. But Ruth was already an icon.

I had a stable full of cheap claiming horses with me and I had shipped the horses from a training center in Lexington, Kentucky. It was hot. I was exhausted from the strain of trying to do everything right. The security guard told me no stall space had been reserved for my stable and I couldn't unload. The horses were sweating and thirsty. They stomped and snorted, rocking the van, while I stomped and snorted around the guard shack. I prayed none would throw themselves down and injure a leg.

A golf cart, groaning under the weight of a huge woman, careened around the corner. There she sat, like a Tahitian queen on her throne, reading the Coggins tests and past racing results on my thoroughbreds. The guard seemed to shrink inside his uniform as she barked, "Let him unload stupid. We've got room and we sure as

155

hell can't run a race meet without horses." When she spoke, her hand caressed the only other rider I ever saw on that cart, a .357 magnum with an extended barrel. Ruth never once looked in my direction.

"Oh, I remember her. She could be a very persuasive woman," I said. "How did she coax you back, Bob?"

"It wasn't hard to talk me into coming back home."

It's odd, and sometimes wonderful, how words or groups of words will awaken your memory, like your mother giving you a gentle shake on a warm Saturday morning. Back home on the track - I hear Bob's voice, but I see my first menial job at Ellis Park in 1976. I was grooming horses for the Dan Wilson Stable. Work started at 5AM seven days a week. We finished by 11AM, giving Dan time to drink several beers before going front side to the races, where he drank vodka tonics all afternoon. By early evening, he was usually ready to delegate feeding and watering to me.

The welfare of twenty expensive horses was exhausting to an irresponsible kid. By 9PM, I was emotionally drained and in my home, in other words, the small wooden "tack shack" at the end of our barn. I slept on horse blankets, hugged by the incense of rolled oats and blackstrap molasses. There were advantages to this arrangement. Dan was generous and easy going. I answered to no one and the money I earned was mine to keep or throw away. It takes years of adult obligations to fully appreciate the value of a circumstance like that one.

"You came back to the track about the time I was leaving," I said.

"Yeah, once it's in your blood, it's like an addiction. You quit doing it but you can't stop thinking about it. I knew I was never going to be physically able to ride races anymore, so working in the front office was the only way for me to keep in touch with jockeys and trainers."

"You've spent the last fifteen years here, Bob. What's the greatest change you've noticed in horseracing, particularly at the smaller tracks like Ellis?"

"That's easy. It's changed from a sport to a business. How can you operate a twenty million dollar facility for only three months a year without some pretty tight business practices? Another thing that really pushed us into the business world was the state of Kentucky legalizing simulcasting. Even though we only have live racing here at

Ellis from July through Labor Day, we can take in revenue the other nine months by giving people the means to bet on horse races all over the U.S. The beauty of it is we don't have to keep a full complement of employees the year around, just a few pari-mutuel clerks and some kitchen help."

I understand the practicality of what Bob has been saying, but it strongly re-enforces my feeling that an era has ended.

"Bob, when I raced here more than fifteen years ago, I was on a first name basis with almost every trainer, jockey, groom and hotwalker on the backside. That familiarity was something that made me love this place. With stables shipping in from every corner of the country, it can't be that way anymore."

"No you're right. It isn't and certainly, that goes to eliminating the strong family atmosphere we once had. But we still work at making all the people on the backside feel safe and appreciated while they're here. The track chaplain has an office above the kitchen area. We've built dorms for the stable help, no more sleeping in tack rooms. We have a softball league and picnics each summer. And these are things we could never have done without extra money."

Bob goes on to explain that, even with recreational programs and a better living environment, backside security still struggles with the drunks. Yet, I can't imagine a racetrack without them. Over the course of ten years as a racetracker, I came in contact with hundreds of people at many of the racetracks in the Midwest; but the ones I've always remembered were the drunks, like you always remember the colors of a rainbow after the storm.

I don't mean the slobbering, obnoxious pseudo - rich drunks, or the once-a-month mint julep drinkers. I'm thinking of the characters that provided the glue that holds my memory of an era together. These old boys considered the racetrack their home and drinking a career choice. Many of them never used a last name. Hoss, Wally, Barrel, and Victor were single named men who all worked for me at one time or another. I paid them cash, usually by the day, to cool out thoroughbreds after a swift morning gallop, or an afternoon race. Sometimes they mucked stalls or wrapped legs, if they were sober enough. None of them ever ventured away from the backside of the racetrack except when riding in a horse van to another track

Each man lived in a tack room. Each had his personal ritual for drinking. Wally hid vodka bottles in hay bales around the barn. It was a game. He would turn a corner, disappearing on the opposite side of the barn, stop the horse, take a long pull on a bottle, and then continue the journey. When I first hired him, I wondered how it was possible to get puking drunk by walking around a barn.

Hoss kept a warm beer by his cot. He awoke at 5AM every morning, and drank the single beer. There was method in this madness. On most mornings, this calmed his nerves enough to pee in the empty beer can, eliminating a cold walk to the urinals. Barrel arrived shortly after 5AM with a washtub full of ice and the cheapest ale on sale at the track kitchen that day.

The most enigmatic of the group was Victor. He smoked Velvet tobacco rolled unevenly in Topps cigarette paper. Once the cigarette was fashioned, Victor attached it to the right corner of his mouth and never removed it. When his lip got warm, he would spit it out and roll another. This wasn't normally a problem unless a load of dry straw was stacked close by. Victor spoke in rapid riddles. The cigarette bounced up and down, like a fishing bobber, in perfect cadence with his words. "If a preacher can save whores, why can't he save me two for Friday night?" "How can a woman be pretty ugly?" "What's under a pony tail?" Those questions served as an excuse to ponder the answers over a sip of bourbon. He asked them aloud frequently while he worked.

A cursory description of these men does them no justice. They were all more than the sum of their parts. Yes, they were alcoholics and their lack of moderation was contagious. Yes, each one had his own personal tragedy by which he excused the drinking. Yet, whiskey was all I ever needed to lock up around them. Integrity and honor were part of their code. You don't steal. You don't lie. You pay what you owe, and you never neglect a racehorse.

I learned important lessons about family in my young manhood from these vagabonds and others like them. I learned what drove my father to succeed and what drove us apart. I began to feel again and to realize that the distance between my father and me had more to do with not understanding our own selves rather than misunderstanding each other. I began to recover some of my life that had been exorcised by nightmares of combat in the Vietnam War.

"Right now, we're planning on an upgrade of our wagering facilities. We want to make the person spending his money happy.

We're also keeping our fingers crossed regarding alternative gaming laws."

"Alternative gaming - what's that?"

"If the state government passes laws that allow it, we'll be able to line our walls with slot machines and other types of gambling devices. That could effectively double our revenue and create more changes for the industry."

I like the fact that Bob calls the current state of racing, an industry. It's easy for me to envision a clear demarcation between the Ellis Park in my memory and the Ellis Park industry of today. I thank Bob for an enlightening interview and ask to drive through the barn area on my way out. He phones ahead to the guard shack and tells them I'm coming.

On the way to my car, I walk past one of the steel beams in the grandstand that has a high water mark on it. Men in boats scratched the mark into the surface during the flood of 1937, when this whole facility was under the Ohio River. I put my back against the beam and stretch upward. The mark is still well over my head. I remember being ten years old again. My father stood me against this same beam so I wouldn't wander off in the crowd while he bought daily double tickets. He said, "There's a time to move and a time to stand still. Now is the time to stand still."

I'm thinking about that simple principle this cold November, even though my father has passed away. Is it possible to make progress by not moving? I think the answer is yes.

ABOUT JIM MCGARRAH

Marine, social worker, carpet layer, janitor, bartender, race horse trainer, and college professor, Jim McGarrah lives in Louisville, Kentucky, close enough to Churchill Downs to hear the crowd roar each year at the Kentucky Derby.

Jim McGarrah's poems, essays, and stories appear frequently in literary journals such as *Bayou Magazine, Breakwater, Cincinnati Review, Chamber Four, Connecticut Review,* and *North American Review.* He is the author of three award-winning books of poetry: *Running the Voodoo Down* (Elixir Press, 2003); *When the Stars Go Dark* (Main Street Rag, 2009); and *Breakfast at Denny's* (Ink Brush Press, 2013). His memoir of war, *A Temporary Sort of Peace* (Indiana Historical Society Press, 2007) won the national Eric Hoffer Legacy Non-Fiction Award, and the sequel, *The End of an Era,* was published in 2011. He is editor, along with Tom Watson, of the anthology *Home Again: Essays and Memoirs from Indiana* and the former managing editor of *Southern Indiana Review.*

47270928R10098

Made in the USA
Charleston, SC
07 October 2015